Sophia Orne Johnson

Every Woman Her Own Flower Gardener

A Handy Manual of Flower Gardening for Ladies. Fourth Edition

Sophia Orne Johnson

Every Woman Her Own Flower Gardener
A Handy Manual of Flower Gardening for Ladies. Fourth Edition

ISBN/EAN: 9783337068202

Printed in Europe, USA, Canada, Australia, Japan

Cover: Foto ©Lupo / pixelio.de

More available books at **www.hansebooks.com**

EVERY WOMAN

HER OWN

𝔉lower 𝔊ardener.

A HANDY MANUAL OF

FLOWER GARDENING FOR LADIES.

By Mrs. S. O. JOHNSON.
("DAISY EYEBRIGHT.")

FOURTH EDITION.

NEW YORK:
HENRY T. WILLIAMS, - - - PUBLISHER.
Office of the Horticulturist.
1874.

Entered according to Act of Congress, in the year eighteen hundred and seventy-one, by
HENRY T. WILLIAMS,
in the office of the Librarian of Congress, at Washington, D. C.

VAN BENTHUYSEN PRINTING HOUSE,
Stereotypers and Printers,
Albany, N. Y.

CONTENTS.

CHAPTER I.
The Flower Garden—Its Uses, etc. 5

CHAPTER II.
Construction of Beds—Beds in Lawn—Ribbon Gardening—Rockeries—Directions for Massing Flowers—Diagrams for laying out Gardens 12

CHAPTER III.
Annuals—Their Culture and Varieties—A List of the Most Desirable for Amateur Gardeners 18

CHAPTER IV.
Perennials—Biennials—Their Treatment, etc.—Lists of Most Desirable Varieties..... 27

V.
Geraniums—Pelargoniums—The Difference between the two Plants—Their Culture and Varieties—Double Geraniums—The Zonale Geraniums—The Liliputian Tribe—Lists of Desirables and Novelties.. 32

CHAPTER VI.
Bedding out Plants—Pansies—Verbenas—Heliotropes—Feverfews, etc............... 38

CHAPTER VII.
The Fuchsia.. 47

CHAPTER VIII.
The Cultivation of the Rose 52

CHAPTER IX.
Ornamental Vines.. 62

CHAPTER X.
Ornamental Shrubs for Garden and Lawn 69

CHAPTER XI.
The Carnation and Picotee Pinks 73

CHAPTER XII.
Herbaceous Plants—Pæonies—Phloxes—Chrysanthemums—Delphiniums—and a Select List of Desirable Herbaceous Flowers 77

CHAPTER XIII.
Immortelles, or Everlasting Flowers and Ornamental Grasses—Acroliniums—Globe Amaranths—Helicrysums—Helipterium Sanfordii—Rodanthes—Xeranthemums—and a Select List of Grasses, Annual and Perennial 83

CHAPTER XIV.
Ornamental Foliaged Plants — Coleus —Achyranthus — Caladiums — Silver Leaved Plants—Cannas, etc.—Tri-colored Geraniums, Gold and Silver Edged 89

CHAPTER XV.
Summer Flowering Bulbs—Japan Lilies—Gladiolus—Dahlias—Vallota, etc. 96

CHAPTER XVI.
Spring Flowering Bulbs—Snowdrops—Crocuses—Hyacinths—Tulips—Daffodils—Jonquils—Narcissus—Polyanthus Narcissus—Lilies of the Valley, etc. 107

CHAPTER XVII.
Old Fashioned Flowers 119

CHAPTER XVIII.
Vegetables and Hotbeds 122

CHAPTER XIX.
Arrangement of Bouquets, Vases, etc.—Flowers in Churches 132

CHAPTER XX.
General Management of the Garden—The Soil—Selection of Seeds—Weeding—Watering—Planting out—Pruning, etc.—Saving of Seeds—Preparing Pots—Taking up and Preserving Flowers in Winter—Sleep of Flowers—Insects—Cultivate the Beautiful everywhere—Lines of Mrs. Howitts—Let us Teach our Children to Love Flowers rather than Fashion 139

CHAPTER I.

THE FLOWER-GARDEN—ITS ROMANCE AND REALITY.

> "There's not a flower can grow upon the earth
> Without a flower upon the spiritual side;
> All that we see is pattern of what shall be in the mount,
> Related royally, and built up to eterne significance.
>   There's nothing small;
> No lily, muffled hum of summer bee,
> But finds its coupling in the spinning stars;
> No pebble at your feet but proves a sphere;
> No chaffinch but implies a cherubim;
>   Earth is full of heaven,
> And every common bush a-fire with God."

A beautiful garden, tastefully laid out, and well kept, is a certain evidence of taste, refinement and culture. It makes a lowly cottage attractive, and lends a charm to the stateliest palace.

An English writer, lately visiting our country, writes: "I can conceive of nothing more dreary than to live in the country and have no garden. To have no garden is to take the poetry, and nearly all the charms away from country life. To have a garden, is to have many friends continually near.

"What a difference between what Mr. Carlyle calls an 'umbrageous man's rest, in which a king might wish to sit and smoke, and call it his,' with its roses, and honeysuckles, and fuchsias clambering in through the very windows in crowds, and the dreary, arid prospect around thousands of American houses!"

This hardly seems a fair criticism upon our homes. Having been an enthusiastic lover of flowers from childhood, and having cultivated them ever since the use of the hands was learned, I cannot recognize its truth;—have never known of many such houses, as he describes. Yet many American writers will declare that slender porticos, fanciful verandas, sculptured gables, and deep bay windows are often seen in this country, without a vestige of a flower or climbing vine about them; while in England, the poorest laborer's cot is a bower of greenery; and his little plat of flowers, often vies with that of his employer.

It is not always wealth or art that gives to English homes their beauty and picturesqueness, but it is the attention of their inmates, to the cultivation of the *"Green things of the earth."*

It is not the latticed casement nor the high gable that attracts the notice of the traveler, but the brilliant flowers and the trailing vines that drape and embower them.

American women live in-doors too much, and thus sacrifice their health and spirits. They cultivate neuralgia, dyspepsia, and all their attendant ills—rather than the beautiful and glorious flowers which God has scattered so abundantly all over the world.

This little pamphlet is written for the purpose of coaxing them to come out into the sunshine, and begging them to

"List to Nature's teachings."

A little garden, all one's own, is a real Eden! Earth possesses no greater charm; and there is no cosmetic equal to the fresh, sweet morning air, and the cheerful sunshine.

You can make no investment which will give you such interest; health, happiness, and pure enjoyment will be the coin in which it is paid; and the returns are not made semi-annually, but daily.

With what intense delight one watches the first tiny leaves of the seeds one has planted; and what pleasure one takes in the unfolding of the first flower! A grand garden cared for by a gardener, can never give its possessor as much delight as one in which nearly all the work is done by one's own hands.

To be sure, Pat O'Shovelem's aid is needful to prepare the ground, lay out the beds, and harden the walks; but, gentler, smaller hands can plant the seeds and roots, can keep down the weeds, tie up, stake, train, water and prune.

I have little faith in American women becoming farmers,—holding the plow—wielding the spade or the shovel; but I do know from long experience, that all the rest of the work can be accomplished by women, if they possess a love for the beautiful. There lies the trouble; few of our children are taught to garden; if they possess a natural taste for the pursuit, sometimes it is gratified, but not always.

Mrs. Japonica and Miss McFlimsey hold up their hands in holy horror at the very idea of any of their kindred soiling their hands with the work.

"Flora work among her namesakes!" they exclaim; "forbid it all Japonicadom!"

Yet how much harder do they work at the crowded party or ball! To dance the "German," requires quite as much physical strength as to plant a flower-garden, and rake off the weeds;—but that is the fashion, and beef tea and stimulants must be resorted to, to sustain the feeble knees, uplift the nerveless fingers. Women can find strength to cultivate a garden successfully, if they will commence by degrees. If their muscles and sinews are not accustomed to the work, they will soon rebel against it when forced to attend to it for several hours at once.

Garden by degrees, my friends, and cultivate your muscles, with your plants!

An hour, or even half an hour, is long enough for a commencement, and the next day extend the time ten minutes, and so on, until you can work for three, or even six hours in succession.

But take it easy; provide an old piece of carpeting to kneel upon while planting, or weeding with a fork; and if your knees are not accustomed to that position, humor them by placing an empty raisin or soap box upon the carpet, and sit upon that;—and if a cushion would also be agreeable, cover a small pillow with some dark chintz, and place that on the box. Now you will have a luxurious seat, and can garden without a sense of pain; yet *don't stay too long, nor become too much heated.* The carpeting protects the skirts from the dampness of the soil, and should always be used. It can be kept conveniently at hand, with the box and the cushion.

Of course, flounces, puffs, and furbelows, with their accompanying upper skirts, are not suitable for such occupations. A dark chintz dress is the best, for it can go into the wash-tub when it is in need of cleansing. A woolen bathing dress makes an excellent garden costume

—for skirts are always in the way. If it is admissible on the beach, where wealth and fashion do congregate, why not in the garden, surrounding one's house?

A large shade hat, and a pair of old kid gloves are indispensable. Rubber gloves are often recommended, but are far too clumsy for the fingers.

Now, the dress is bespoken, and we must purchase the tools required. A large three-pronged iron fork, with a short handle, is needful for loosening the ground, removing plants and uprooting weeds. I should rather do without a trowel than such a fork. They can be purchased of all hardware dealers.

A small set of tools, comprising a rake and hoe on one handle, a trowel, and a spade, are very essential. With their aid much light work can be accomplished without calling upon Mr. O'Shovelem.

A watering pot, with a large nozzle, and a fine sprinkler, is also required.

With these implements, *every woman can be her own gardener*—and not only raise all the flowers she may desire, but also contribute a large share of the vegetables that are always welcomed at the table, during both summer and winter.

The cultivation of the soil possesses a wonderful fascination; its very odor, after a refreshing shower, is inspiring; and as you gather your flowers, you will also gather improvement in many ways.

"He made them all, and what He designs, can ne'er be deemed unworthy of our study, and our love." If we see a pot of flowers in a window, it gives us respect for the inmates of the dwelling—but if we see a beauteous garden, "*A brilliant carpet of unnumbered dyes,*" we know that there is taste and refinement within that home.

On the European continent, women work in the fields with the men, and become beasts of burden. I hope never to see them thus, in this more favored land, but I do desire to have them take a daily interval from the labor and care of the house, and breathe into their hearts the oxygen and iron contained in the fresh air; taste the balm and the tonic of the sunlight and the garden.

Every day there is some work to be done, if the garden is well kept. There is no need of having a "*weeding-day,*" like a "*washing-day,*"—for the weeds can be kept down, daily. Every morning dig over one or two beds, according to their size,—and continue the work until all are cleaned up. Then commence again, and thus prevent the soil from becoming baked; and let the air and moisture enter the earth, and nourish the tender roots.

That is my way of gardening. After the beds are made, the walks prepared, no man's hand or foot enters the sacred precinct, excepting to admire, and to receive the flowers.

In the early spring time a half hour may suffice to exhaust the little strength one possesses, but before October comes, with its autumnal glories, several hours can be passed in out-door work without much sense of fatigue.

All the delights of a garden are not comprised in gathering nosegays, and arranging bouquets, vases or festal garlands;—there is great enjoyment in watching the vegetating of the seeds; the developing of the tiny leaves, the forming of the minute buds—and then comes at last—

"The bright, consummate flower!"

Floriculture has been called the gem of all cultures. Its influence makes us more courteous, if not more intelligent; and what can we find in nature so emblematical of bloom, decay, and death?

It has been said that "as domestic floriculture and gardening has been the inclination of beings, and the choice of philosophers, so it has been the favorite of public and private men, a pleasure of the greatest, and the care of the meanest: and indeed an employment and a possession, for which no man is too high nor too low. Flowers are the relics of Eden's bowers."

And there is no pastime that can give as much pleasure, with so small an expenditure. Gray, the poet, and also a skillful naturalist, tells us that the enjoyment of life depends upon "having always something going forward;" and exclaims: "*Happy are they who can create a rose-tree, or erect a honeysuckle!*"

It is indeed this very "*having always something going forward*" that produces the enjoyment experienced by the amateur gardener; the glory and fragrance of the flowers forming the crowning gratification. There is a pride—a most pleasing pride—in culling a bouquet for a friend, from flowers raised by one's own hand.

The creation of a beautiful object is certainly "*a great fact,*" of which any of us may be justly and honestly proud.

Few of us possess the talent to transfer and perpetuate on canvas, or in marble, the glorious hues and forms of nature, but the lowest and humblest can raise flowers which Solomon, in all his glory, could not have eclipsed!

Why does not everybody have a *Geranium*, a *Rose*, a *Fuchsia*, or some other flower in a window, if they do not own land enough to plant a garden? They are very cheap—next to nothing, if raised from a cutting, and of small price if purchased from the florist; and there is companionship in them, as well as grace and beauty.

Charming Leigh Hunt, whom I love to quote, says:

"Flowers sweeten the air, rejoice the eye, link you with nature and innocence, and are something to love. If they cannot love you in return, they cannot hate you; cannot utter hateful words even if neglected; for, though they are all beauty, they possess no vanity; and living, as they do, to do you good, and afford you pleasure, how can you neglect them!"

There are few dwellers in the country who are so destitute as not to be able to indulge in a love for flowers. The garden may be of the smallest size—a mere tiny circle—and it will often be loved the more for its smallness, and receive more care and attention.

It will not do to care for it a week, and then neglect it for two weeks. It demands constant care, daily attendance, waterings, and weedings.

Nothing destroys its beauty like the noxious weeds that will grow up, like Jonah's gourd, if not constantly uprooted. The tenacity of their life is wonderful; uprooting will not always kill them, and they will mature their seeds, and prepare for another struggle with you in an ensuing summer, even when their roots lie withering in the sun. "What hidden virtue is in these things, that it is granted to sow themselves with the wind, and to grapple the earth with this unmitigable stubbornness, and to flourish in spite of obstacles, and never to suffer blight beneath any sun or shade, but always to mock their enemies, with the same wicked luxuriance?"

Thus enquires Hawthorne, while sturdily waging a warfare against them, in the garden of the "Old Manse," at Concord, Mass., and no one can "make reply." Animal manures, though very stimulating to vegetable life, are the sources whence many of the grassy weeds spring. Artificial manures do not introduce so many of these pests into the beds and borders, yet some of them are so highly charged with noxious exhalations that one dislikes to apply them.

Mineral fertilizers are not open to these objections, and I have found them preferable to others on that account.

Guano is always beneficial, if not applied in too large quantities. An iron spoonful of it dug into the ground two or three inches from the stems of the plants will increase their growth and beauty. A less quantity should be given to tender annuals, and small plants.

Liquid animal manures are also easily applied, and give to the plant an immediate stimulant. In pouring it on, avoid touching the leaves or the stems of the plants, but give the earth a copious supply of a weak solution. Guano applied in this manner is very beneficial. I have used all of these with decided success; and always feed my garden bountifully; and receive in return a bountiful supply of flowers and vegetables.

Plant with care and skill; water when needful; feed plenty of nourishment; keep clear from all weeds; tie, stake, prune and cultivate daily, and you will never regret the small investment required to commence and continue a garden; but will become more and more enamored with the occupation; and will yearly increase your stock, and multiply your labors, and will be ready to say with Thomson, the poet of nature:

"I care not, Fortune, what you me deny,
You cannot rob me of free Nature's grace;
You cannot shut the windows of the sky,
Through which Aurora shows her brightening face;
You cannot bar my constant feet to trace
The woods and lawns by living streams at eve:
Let health my nerves and finer fibres brace,
And I their toys to the great children leave;
Of fancy, reason, virtue, nought can me bereave."

CHAPTER II.

CONSTRUCTION OF BEDS, BEDS IN LAWN, RIBBON GARDENING, ROCKERIES.

"Oh! who can speak his joys, when Spring's young morn,
From wood and pasture open'd on his view;
When tender green buds blush upon the thorn,
And the first primrose dips its leaves in dew."

In preparing gardens to receive our flowers, it is better to avoid raised beds, with deep walks. They suffer from the intense heat of our summers; and the rains wash them down, often exposing the roots of the plants. Grass edgings are objectionable, on account of the labor required to keep the sods from spreading.

Beds that are artistically cut in the grass-plat produce a better effect; and the brilliant hues of the flowers contrast perfectly with the soft, shaven, emerald tint of the grass. One of the most attractive features about a house, is a garden tastefully cut in the lawn. It is open to but one objection—the dew upon the grass makes it rather unapproachable in the early morning, when its owner desires to feast her eyes upon its beauties.

Three designs are given for cutting beds in the grassy lawn, and an artistic eye will enable our gardeners to vary them as they please. The walks can be well trodden down, and hardened with sifted coal ashes or clay. Gravel is not so desirable, as it clings to the feet. The grass can be left between the beds, or cut out, but if the latter is done, they can receive more care in the early hours of the day.

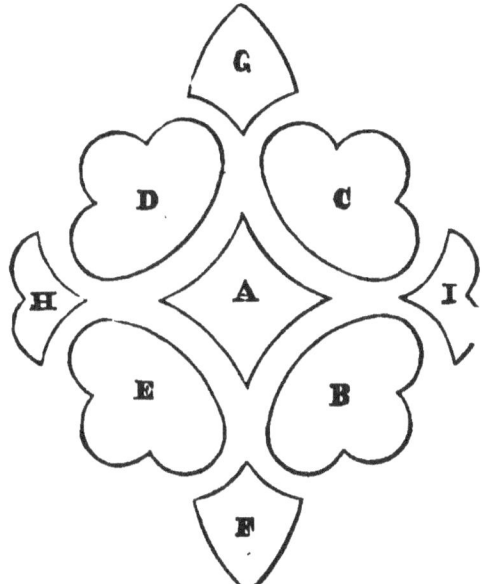

DIAGRAM No. 1

center, A, place a stocky plant of Scarlet Salvia; at B, Scarlet Geraniums; D, White Geranium; C, Heliotropes; E, Carnations; G, Asters; F, Zinnias; H and I, Stocks.

DIAGRAM No. 2.

A, Ricinus, Sanvitalia procumbens round it; B, Scarlet Verbenas; C, White Verbenas; D, Purple; E, Striped, Pink and White; F, Richest Crimson; G, Pure White; H, Brightest Pink; I, Darkest Maroon. The outer beds can be each of one kind of plant, *Heliotropes, Carnations, Geraniums, Pelargoniums, Asters, Balsams, Zinnias,* and *Stocks,* or any flowers that suit the owner's taste.

DIAGRAM No 3.

In the center mound, plant a fine specimen of Arundo donax, or one of the Pampas Grass. In each of the pear-shaped beds, put a different colored geranium, the tallest species at the stem end, and the Tom Thumb varieties at the broadest edge. In the circles plant some white flowers that will retain their beauty. In the crescents, brilliant scarlet flowers; and in the bordering of the half moon, either try ribbon gardening, or fill up with a mosaic in squares of scarlet, white, purple, orange, blue, bright pink, crimson, and all the numberless shades that flowers afford. These beds furnish a great scope for exercising one's taste in arranging colors; and very brilliant effects may be produced without a great outlay of time or money.

The crescent-shaped garden can be approached from the main walk, and if the walks are hardened with ashes, it can be easily tended. All flower beds should be dug a foot deep; well enriched with animal or mineral manures; the lumps all finely pulverized, and the surface of the beds raked as smoothly as possible.

Portulacca, Nemophila, Thrift, Gypsophila and *Dwarf Asters* make very pretty edgings.

Ribbon Gardening.

Flowers may be planted in ribbon fashion, that is, by employing those of primary colors, and arranging them with the tallest for the background, or in the center. If sowed in a circular bed, be sure to have a brilliant scarlet or white flower in the center, which should be taller than all the rest. A Scarlet Geranium (*Gen. Grant*), for the center, White Feverfew surrounding that; Blue Larkspur should come next; Yellow Calceolarias next; and then the Dwarf Asters, of a rich crimson color, bordering on purple, would contrast well. For borderings to the plans given in this chapter, the Hyacinth-flowered Stocks would ribbon beautifully. Plant a row of the Scarlet, then White, next Lilac, then Canary Colored, then Bright Pink. They will grow to the same height, and produce a fine effect. Verbenas are also excellent for this purpose, and can be planted in concentric circles or in parallelograms, with six or seven colors, arranging them as a rainbow. A narrow semi-circle thus planted could be called the rainbow garden. Phlox Drummondii, Candytuft, Lobelias and Zonale Geraniums can all be employed in ribbon gardening. Take care to arrange the colors with vivid contrasts —orange and purple, white and scarlet, but do not let blue and purple mingle. The arrangement of the ribboning must depend, of course, upon the stock of plants you possess, and after one year's trial you will, doubtless, succeed in producing a fine effect. The only requisite rules are, to arrange the plants according to their height and coloring, always planting the outer edges with some dwarf plant that contrasts strongly. The *Alternantheras*, ornamental foliaged plants that grow but four or five inches high, are unsurpassed for edgings. They will receive due attention in the chapter devoted to Variegated Leaved Plants.

For planting in masses of coloring, *Truffanto Asters, Smith's Prize Balsam, Dianthus florepleno, Linum coccineum, Schizanthus atropurpureus, Calceolaria* and *Centranthus macrosiphon* make a fine show. Plant a small bed of each.

A bed of miniature flowers is always charming. *Lobelia marmorata, Leptosiphon hybridus, Clintonia azurea grandiflora, Fenzleria dianthiflora* and *Grammanthes gentianoides* are all dwarfs, and planted together with a bordering of *Gypsophylla muralis*, the effect is lovely! A bed of *Mignonette* is indispensable, and it will flourish in the shade, and in damp places, blooming luxuriantly.

Rockeries.

There are many plants which thrive much better in a sheltered, rocky situation, and thence has sprung up the fashion for constructing "Rockeries." Or it happens that some large rocks crop out on a portion of ground which is within view of the house, and it is desirable to ornament them. In the latter case, you have only to plant strong growing vines with large foliage, such as the Wild Grape Vine; the Clematis, or Virgin's Bower, that trails its white, starry blossoms, and its puffy, wooly seed pods all over the forests of this country. These two vines will render the offending rocks most picturesque. Southern ladies can entwine among them the lovely Yellow Jessamine of their woods, which throws a golden hue over all their forests. The *Ampelopsis* (or Virginia Creeper), or Five Fingered Ivy, and the *Aristolochia* (or Dutchman's Pipe), are also desirable for this purpose; also the *Periplo cagræca*, or Silk Vine of the Southern States.

One, or all of these vines, will soon render the obnoxious rocks a joy forever! Artificial Rockeries are usually constructed of stones of various sizes, with the soil firmly embedded betwixt them. They can be made very easily from the clinkers of the coal furnace. If large pieces can be obtained, whitewash some of them to increase their picturesqueness. Boulders, stones from brooks, or hill sides, can all be used advantageously.

Commence with the largest-sized stones, and build it up in an irregular, jagged shape to imitate nature. A Rockery can be made as a receptacle of Mineralogical Specimens, which would increase its value.

If you send to the woods and brooks for the stones, bring the soil thence, and, if not rich enough, add a little compost. but native Ferns and Vines do not require a large supply of stimulants. Plant the Ferns and Mosses on the shadiest side, and trail over the stones small vines, like the *Lysimachia numerlaria,* Vinca, minor and major, Moneywort, Lobelias, varieties of the Sedums, and the various Annuals mentioned under that head, as desirable for rock work. The varieties of the Saxifragora, with their broad leaves, and large clusters of bright pink or red flowers, are very effective among the trailing vines and ferns.

A small Evergreen tree will show to advantage from some rocky point.

The Alpine Plants are also lovely for such constructions.

Crocus bulbs can be planted among the smaller stones, and in the early Spring will make a fine show. After they have bloomed, their places can be filled with Dwarf Asters and Dwarf Stocks, Phlox Drummondii and Pinks.

Rockeries can be rendered very ornamental additions to the lawn or shrubbery, but they require a tasteful eye to construct them, and a loving hand to tend them; without these they can never be eye-sweet.

CHAPTER III.

ANNUALS—THEIR CULTURE AND TREATMENT.

"Come, ye soft sylphs,
Teach the fine seed, instinct with life, to shoot
In earth's cold bosom, its descending root;
With pith elastic, stretch its rising stem,
Part the twin lobes, expand the throbbing gem;
Clasp in your airy arms the aspiring plume,
Fan with your balmy breath its kindling bloom;
Each widening scale, and bursting film unfold,
Swell the green cup, and tint the flower with gold."

Annuals are considered the chief ornaments of the flower garden throughout the summer and autumn, and many of them are desirable for house culture.

They have great claims upon our attention, and should be more extensively cultivated in every garden. It is impossible to plant, in a private plat of ground, all the kinds and varieties that are offered to us in the Seedsmen's Catalogues, but a judicious selection of the best kinds will give a charming assortment of brilliant flowers.

It is almost superfluous to mention that *annuals* are plants which spring from seed, and perfect their growth and seed, and perish with the autumn; though their life may be prolonged by cutting off the flowers, not allowing the seed-pods to form, and keeping them housed in the winter.

They are divided into hardy; half-hardy and tender; and are natives of various lands. Many of them have been greatly improved, by the care and patience of the florist, from their normal state, and transformed into flowers of the most gorgeous hues, and the most perfect shape.

Asters, Balsams, Larkspurs, Petunias, Portulaccas, Stocks and *Zinnias* have all become exceedingly double and of every brilliant hue; while many others have had their flowers much increased in size, and otherwise improved.

These flowers are more generally cultivated than any other class of flowers, and they, alike, adorn the yard of the cottage, and the *parterre* of the palace.

They will grow almost anywhere, and in any kind of soil, but thrive much better if heed is paid to their wants, and they are provided with a sunny location, well drained, and are well supplied with rich sandy loam; though there are some kinds which prefer a clayey soil. There are only a few which require a very rich soil, yet, most of them will reward you with a brighter show of flowers if well fed. It does not pay to starve plants, any more than to starve animals.

It is very desirable to locate your garden where it can be in constant view from the windows of the house; flowers are our bosom friends and we desire to have them always in sight; when weary they refresh one, when happy they add to one's happiness, and when sad and gloomy they give to one pleasant thoughts, smooth the care-worn brow, and uplift the heart to the Giver of all good things.

To prepare the soil, let Mr. O'Shovelem dig up the grass-plat, if needful, and prepare the beds in front of the piazza, porch or sitting room, if it has a southeast direction; if not, take the next best, a southwestern location. Few plants will thrive well in a northern exposure, though Pansies love the shade, and will flourish there. If you can procure a compost of sand (not sea sand), leaf mould, loam and manure—a quarter of each—you will have as good soil as you can desire; but if not within reach, take what offers, and if it is heavy and stiff, add sand to lighten it; if friable and light, add ashes, muck or soil from old pastures, taken from under the sods. This is always desirable. Sand is also an essential.

Laying out the Beds.

Have the garden well spaded over, and then lay out the beds. If you have a geometrical eye, you can mark out circles, semi-circles, triangles, stars, diamonds and all sorts of curved beds; and if you can have all the assistance you desire from "men-folks," border their edges with narrow strips of turf, which must be kept closely shaven, and not allowed to encroach upon the beds.

If you depend upon your own exertions, avoid the turf; for it exacts too much hard muscular work for women to encounter.

A bordering is now manufactured of Terra Cotta, which is highly praised; and it is said to withstand the frost and snow of the coldest regions. The Drain Pipe and Terra Cotta works in New York, make several styles. Tiles are also introduced with good effect. Box edgings are always tasteful and pretty. If you can possess none of these, you can, at least, border the beds with Dwarf Annuals and Perennials. The Tom Thumb plants of every kind are very pretty for this purpose; the stone-crop and, indeed, all the varieties of Sedums, make effective edgings. *Gypsophila muralis* is also beautiful for an edging, and its spray-like flowers are indispensable for both vase and bouquet. They cover the flowers like a mist, increasing their charms by partly veiling them.

Sowing the Seed, etc.

The hardy varieties, like *Candytuft, Phlox Drummondii, Sweet Alyssum, Sweet Peas*, etc., can be sown as soon as the ground becomes a little warm, and the weather is in a degree settled. Indeed, all these kinds, and many others, will bloom earlier in the summer if they are planted in the autumn. The frost and snow does not disturb their rest. *Sweet Peas* are very essential for all gardens. Their fragance is grateful to all; and a bunch of the new colored ones, mingled with the old favorites, equals the soft and liquid tints of the sunset cloud. But don't put *Scarlet Geraniums* or *Verbenas* among them; their vivid hues will pale and dim the beauteous Peas.

They bloom much more profusely, if planted four or five inches in depth, and are not so apt to mildew.

The half-hardy annuals should not be sown, excepting in the South, before the middle of May; and the tender ones, not until June, if one desires good success in their vegetation and growth.

A large amount of vexation might be avoided if amateur florists would pay a little heed to natural laws.

For both half-hardy and tender Annuals, planting in-doors, or under glass, is very needful. If this is done, they can be brought forward so as to bloom by the last of June, or the first of July, and one is fully repaid for the extra trouble by their graceful, lovely flowers. All these varieties of Annuals require transplanting. No *Aster, Petunia, Stock* or *Zinnia* will show its beauty if not allowed plenty of room in which to grow and bloom. So, it is as well to transplant them from boxes, or hotbeds, early in the summer, when all fear of frost is past, as to do it later from the garden beds.

Seeds of various sizes require different depths of covering. The smaller the seed, the less the soil it needs to plant it, and the finer the soil should be.

Portulaccas, Petunias, and all tiny seeds, should be mixed with sand, and sprinkled or sifted on to the earth prepared for them, and then gently pressed down with the flat of the trowel or the hoe. The general rule for planting has been to the depth of three times the diameter of the seed.

Too deep planting is a fruitful source of the usual loss of seeds, so much complained of by amateur gardeners.

The several essentials to successful germination of seeds of all kinds are suitable soil, suitable moisture and warmth; if these are in excess, or not sufficient, some, if not all, of the seeds will fail.

In planting seeds in the open border, the soil must be thoroughly pulverized, no little lumps left in it to destroy plant life.

Rake in the seeds, scattering them thinly around; or, a better way is to tie a string to two small sticks; plant one of them firmly in the earth, and with the other draw a circle of the dimensions you may desire; wind up the string until you have it of the right length, then plant the seeds in the circle, and label them. Don't trust to your memory for the names, and then say "this pink flower, that red one, and the other blue or yellow one," but learn their names, and call them by them.

One often rebels at the many-syllabled word that is applied to a tiny mite of a flower; yet, that same Latin word tells to every botanist its class and order, while the common, familiar, local name is recognized only by one language.

Miss Mitford says: "One is never thoroughly sociable with flowers until they are naturalized, as it were, christened, provided with decent, homely, well-wearing English names."

The practice of giving Latin names to flowers and plants has been styled pedantic. It is not so; for it conveys an idea of the flower to every student of Botany and Gardening in every nation.

Leigh Hunt thus writes upon the names of flowers:

"Pink is not by itself a pretty name, but we have associated it since our first dawnings of infancy, with the sweetness of the flower, so now the name and flower are one, and the poor monosyllable becomes rich in sweetness and appropriateness."

And again:

"*Browallia* is a pretty name, and was given to a Peruvian flower by Linnæus in honor of a friend of his by the name of Browall; yet the name gives no idea of the flower which is remarkably attractive;" and, he suggests that *Browall's Beauty* would have immortalized both the friend and the flower, and have advertised its claims to the regard of the florist.

A short digression from seed planting, fair friends. which it is to be hoped you will pardon and overlook.

When your seeds are planted, unless the day is cloudy and showery, they will require shading from the heat of the sun.

I find old newspapers are the best protection; but, if the patches are small, flower pots can be inverted over them. The newspapers must be laid over the seeds, after they have been well watered, and fastened at the corners by small stones or a handful of the earth. At night they should be removed to let the dew moisten the ground, and put back before it is dried up in the morning. Continue this until the tiny leaflets appear; then remove them entirely. If the ground is dry the seeds must be thoroughly wet every night. Moisture is very needful to germinate seeds; without its aid they cannot sprout. The would-be florists often plant their seeds as the Catalogues direct and then give no farther heed to them. You will often hear it said, "I can't make annuals grow. I planted fifty to sixty varieties, and not half a dozen of them ever sprouted. I have no faith in the seedsmen; they send out old seeds and keep all the new for their own gardens."

"Did you water them well, and shade them from the noontide heat?" is asked. "Why, no! I never thought of that. I planted them, and supposed that was enough."

My fair friends, unless the clouds favor you and drop rain, or hide the sun for three or four days, your seeds will become baked and shriveled, and you cannot expect them to grow.

The thin-skinned seeds will germinate most quickly, while those that are shrouded in horny textures, vegetate more slowly. It is always well to soak all such seeds. Verbena seeds require twenty-four hours soaking in warm water, and the seeds of the lovely, graceful Cypress vine will not germinate unless boiling water is poured upon them.

Transplanting Seedlings.

When the tiny plants have put forth the fourth or fifth leaf, it is time to provide them with permanent homes. If this is done in the early morning of a warm day—or even later in the forenoon—you may be sure that you will lose your plants. But select a showery, cloudy day, following a dry season, or plant after night-fall, and then water, and shade from the sun of the next day, and you will hardly lose one plant, or even have a leaf curl.

Annuals of most kinds must have plenty of space to grow in. There are few that are not improved by transplanting. Salpiglossis will grow to better advantage thickly planted; also, Erysimum Peroffskianum, whose brilliant orange flowers render it desirable to every garden. Mignonette, Larkspurs and Poppies will not bear transplanting; they grow from a tap root, and do not easily attach themselves to a new home after their growth is once started.

If Annuals are not planted anew after germinating, their growth is weak and spindling, and they soon cease flowering; while, on the other hand, they will grow luxuriantly, and blossom until the frost withers their fair bloom, if their quarters are ample. Asters should be planted a foot asunder each way; and Stocks, Balsams, Zinnias and Petunias require as much room, if not more, to bring them to a state of perfection; and, if mulched with fine manure early in July, they will bloom magnificently.

What Shall We Plant?

This is the query of many women who examine the Illustrated Catalogues, and are not familiar with the high-sounding names, and, therefore, totally at loss to know what are desirable and needful out of the thousands of varieties, illustrated and described therein.

I will give a list of those whose beauties are familiar to me, and whose names are household words:

Asters, Truffauts, Rose Asters, Imbrique, Pompone, Chrysanthemum Flowered, Bouquet, in all their varied colorings and shapes. No garden can afford to be without one or all of these varieties; and they take chief rank in the tribe of Annuals.

Amaranthus melancholicus, variegated leaves.
Anagallis.
Abrobra, a lovely climber.
Abronia, very effective for rock-work.

Ageratum, lavender blue and white.
Acroclinium, white and pink.
Balsams, Smith's Prize and Camellia flowered.
Bartonia aurea, golden yellow.
Browallia, blue with white center, white.
Cacalia, orange scarlet, and yellow.
Calandrinia, crimson, white, pink and lilac.
Coreopsis Burridgii, and coronata.
Canary Bird Flower, beautiful vine.
Candytuft, white, purple and crimson.
Celosia spicata rosea, everlasting flower.
Centranthus, white, flesh colored and pink.
Cerastium, ornamental foliage, for edgings on rock-work.
Chlora grandiflora, bright orange changing to red.
Chrysanthemum coronarium, flore pleno.
Clarkia integripetela, magenta crimson, rich.
Clianthus Dampierii.
Clintonia azurea grandiflora, desirable for rock-work and baskets.
Cobæa scandens, a climber of rapid growth.
Collinsia, various colors, pretty for ribbon borders.
Convolvulus aureus superbus, a golden yellow variety.
Convolvulus mauritanicus, perfect for roses and baskets
Cyanus (Ladies' Delight).
Cypress Vine, the most graceful of climbers.
Eschscholtzia Californica, several colors.
Euphorbia variegata.
Fenzlia, dwarf growth, effective in rustic decorations.
Gilia, various colors.
Godetia, useful in ribbons.
Gypsophylla muralis and elegans.
Helliophila araboides, bright blue, useful for edgings.
Inopsidium acaule, sky blue, loves the shade.
Ipomœa hederacea superba, a beautiful vine.
Kaulfussia atroviolacea.
Larkspur (Hyacinth flowered).
Leptosiphon hybridus, dwarf edgings.
Linum, in several colors.
Lobelia, blue, white and rose color, dwarf.

Lupins, of all colors.
Machæranthera tanaceifolia, bright purple, golden center.
Marigolds, new varieties are very attractive.
Mignonette, Parson's new white and the crimson flowered.
Nasturtiums, of all varieties.
Nemesia compacta elegans.
Nemophila, delicate flowers, very dwarf, love the shade.
Nigella Tonlanesiena.
Oxyura, golden yellow, edged with white.
Sweet Peas of all colors.
Perilla Nankinensis, dark rich foliaged plant.
Phlox Drummondii, of every shade.
Poppy, carnation colored.
Portulacca, double and single.
Ricinus, ornamental foliaged.
Salpiglossis, very beautiful.
Salvia splendens.
Sanvitalia procumbens, suitable for edgings and rock-work.
Saponaria acymoides, lovely for borderings.
Scabiosa (or Mourning Bride), flore pleno.
Schizanthus, all colors.
Statice hybrida.
Stocks, German Dwarf, pyramidal, new hybrid.
Tagetes pumila, marigold of beautiful foliage and flower.
Trifolium (ornamental clover).
Tropæolum, finest mixed varieties.
Viscaria elegans picta.
Vittadina (Australian Daisy), a good edging.
Whitlavia, blue and white.
Zea Japonica (Japanese Maize), ornamental foliage.
Zinnia Elegans, flore pleno, all colors.
Zinnia Mexicana pumila, very double and brilliant.

Among this list of Annuals several climbers have been included; for other species, consult the chapter on Vines and Climbers.

Training and Watering Annuals.

There are few plants that are not benefited by judicious training and pruning.

Balsams are greatly improved by pinching off the side shoots, and allowing only the stalks to grow; or the main shoot may be left to itself, and all the strength of the plant thrown into it, producing an upright stem loaded with gorgeous chalices of bloom. Manure water will increase the size of the flowers, and, thus grown, they make splendid pot plants.

The scissors are useful about many other plants; and their side growth should be checked, and less latitude allowed to their branches.

Zinnias, Stocks and Asters should have the laterals trimmed off; their beauty is improved, if they are kept within bounds.

In watering Annuals, and all flowers, care should be taken to apply it after the sun has set; if water is given in the morning, when the sun is hastening forward to drink up every drop, it is of but little use to the plant; and, if it is given at noon-tide, when the sunbeams fall fiercely hot, it scorches the plants as though Jack Frost had bitten them. The cold drops, falling on the heated surface of the soil, produce the same effect as a chill.

Water slightly warmed to the hand is far more efficacious than that drawn directly from aqueducts or cisterns. If it sets in the sun all day, it will be of the right temperature to apply at night.

English books on gardening, often denounce the practice of frequent watering; but they are no guides for American gardens. Their misty, moisty island, enveloped in clouds, promotes moisture sufficient for their needs; while our heated atmosphere drinks up every drop from the soil. If it has rained during the day the watering pot can hang upon its peg; but if not, its attendance is highly essential for the growth of all tender Annuals, and delicate bedding-out plants.

Many ladies complain of their ill luck in floriculture; no plant thrives with them. Why is this?

Because they neglect the floral darlings. They are assiduous in their attention to them while planting or transplanting them; but then their energy fails; they think that the sun, rain and dew will do the necessary work, and they can rest from their labors.

They never fail to do their appointed work; but you must cultivate in season and out of season if you would raise—

"Bright gems of earth in which, perchance, we see
What Eden was—what Paradise may be."

CHAPTER IV.

PERENNIALS AND BIENNIALS.

"Well they reward the toil.
The sight is pleased, the scent regaled ;
Each opening blossom freely breathes around
Its gratitude, and thanks us with its sweets."

Perennial plants are those which live and blossom through many successive seasons. If planted very early in the border, or brought forward in the hotbed or in window gardens, they bloom the first season, and many of them are hardy enough to withstand the coldest winters of northern New England, while others require protection, and the tender ones must be housed in the cellar to await the return of spring.

Perennials die down every year, but the faithful old roots live, and when the sun awakes them from their wintry sleep, they spring up anew, and delight our senses.

These plants are very deserving of the attention of the amateur florist. They ask but little at one's hands, and will grow and bloom for many years under great neglect. Yet if their roots are not divided, and their food renewed—after a few years they will dwindle away, and finally perish.

Many kinds are raised from seeds. Others by cuttings or increase of the roots; and once in three or four years they require to be taken up, divided, and reset. They flourish best in a light, rich soil.

Dicentra spectabilis, an importation from China, stands at the head of the list for its beauty, grace and hardy qualities. Linnæus knew of its loveliness, and named it *Corydalis formosa*. Mr. Fortune introduced it into England less than twenty years ago, and it has been called *Dilytra, Diclytra,* and *Dicentra,* which are its proper names.

It seeds sparingly, but a white variety has been introduced, whether from seed or from China, I know not. It multiplies rapidly by the roots; the foliage resembles that of a Pæony, and its flowers are rose colored, tipped with white, and hang from long racemes. As a lawn plant, for early spring and summer blooming, it is unsurpassed.

Perennial Flax (*Linum perenne*), is a native from beyond the Mississippi, and is beautiful in color and shape. Its flowers are celestial blue, and they are very abundant. The plant continues in bloom all summer, and is an addition to every garden.

Missouri Evening Primrose (*Œnothera macrocarpa*), also blooms all summer; its flowers are a golden yellow, and the plant is dwarf in habit, but the flowers do not open until the sun's rays are declining.

Petunias are half hardy Perennials, which usually rank with Annuals in the northern part of the United States. They are desirable for the smallest plat of ground—as they grow luxuriantly and flower profusely. They take front rank now, and their curious blotchings and veinings render them very beautiful. The double varieties possess a spicy fragrance, and many of them are as beautifully striped and mottled as a carnation.

Columbines, Lychnis, French Honeysuckles, Phlox, Pinks, Achillea and Campanula are all very beautiful, and if raised from seeds will increase rapidly from the roots.

The Perennial Larkspurs have received great additions to their numbers of late years, and are greatly improved in coloring and the size of the flowers. The blue species possess the most perfect tints—vie with the hues of a cloudless sky!

There are no directions needful for preparing the soil, or planting the seeds, as they are given so fully in the previous chapter.

October is the best month for dividing and transplanting the roots. All perennial plants admit of dividing and transplanting, and it greatly increases the size and beauty of the flowers, and enhances their colors.

The roots of those kinds not found in the seed catalogues, can be purchased at the florist's at slight expense, excepting the rarer kinds and the novelties.

Trees and Shrubs, and nearly all the so-called bedding-out plants, are strictly speaking perennials; yet the term is more particularly applied to those flowers whose stems and leaves annually decay, the roots retaining their vitality. I shall treat more fully of them under the chapter on Pæonies and Herbaceous plants.

I append a list of the most desirable grown from seed:—
Antirrhinum (or Snap-dragon), all colors, hardy.
Aconitum napellus (Monkshood), blue and white, hardy.
Agrostemma hybride flore pleno, hardy.
Alyssum saxatile, golden yellow, hardy.
Aquilegia (Columbine), hardy.
Aralis alpine, hardy.
Armeria splendens (Thrift), half hardy.
Astragalus galegiformis, yellow, hardy.
Aubletia deltoides, hardy, and beautiful for rock work.
Bellis (Double Daisy), half hardy.
Bryonia alba—a trailer, white flowers, hardy.
Calceolarias, half hardy, very beautiful.
Campanula, white, blue, lilac and purple.
Iberis sempervirens, Perennial Candytuft.
Carnations, half hardy, very desirable.
Catananche bicolor, hardy, white, with violet center.
Chelone barbata, hardy perennial.
Chrysanthemum japonicum, very rare.
Commelyne (Spiderwort), half hardy.
Cowslip, hardy.
Datura, half hardy.
Delphinium (Perennial Larkspur).
Dianthus of all kinds, hardy and half hardy.
Digitalis, hardy perennial.
Dodecatheon Meadia, hardy.
Forget-me-not, hardy.
Fraxinella, hardy.
Galega, lilac, white.
Gentiana macrophylla, deep blue.
Guem coccineum (Scarlet Avens), hardy.
Perennial Lupins, hardy.
Everlasting Pea, hardy.
Lavender spica, hardy.
Liatris squarrosa (Blazing Star), a prairie flower.

Lobelia hybridus.
Lychnis haageane, white, red, scarlet.
Mimulus, half hardy.
Pansies.
Papaver (Perennial Poppy).
Penstemnon, white, scarlet, rose, blue, purple.
Petunia.
Phlox decussata.
Phygelius capensis.
Picotee Pink.
Paisley Pink.
Potentilla, golden, crimson, yellow and white.
Sedum (Stonecrop).
Sweet William, Hunt's perfection.
Tritoma uvaria, half hardy.
Verbascum, hardy, white, lilac.
Verbena, half hardy.
Wall flower, very double, half hardy.

Biennials.

These are plants which, like Annuals, generally die after producing their flowers and seeds, but are two years in perfecting these, and in some instances may be induced to flower for two or three successive seasons by preventing them from going to seed; their general culture is the same as for Annuals.

One of the most beautiful is the German Brompton Stock. The greatest improvements have been made in these flowers, and they are now very desirable plants for border or lawn. They are half hardy, will require protection during the winter in northern climates—but will fully repay the care they demand. Any particularly fine plant can be propagated by cuttings, yet they do not always flower as well as those raised from seeds.

Among the Biennials most deserving of culture are:—
Canterbury Bells, double and single varieties, hardy.
Carduus, hardy.
Humea, elegant, half hardy.
Hollyhocks, half hardy.
Hyoscyamus, hardy.

Ipomopsis, half hardy, orange, scarlet, rose.
Silene ornata, hardy biennial.
Silylum elurnium (Ivory Thistle), hardy.
German Stocks, new dwarf bouquet.
Stocks, French winter, or Cocardean.
Scarlet Giant Cape.
Trachelium cœruleum, hardy.

CHAPTER V.

GERANIUMS AND PELARGONIUMS.

*" A brilliant carpet of unnumbered dyes,
With sweet variety enchants the eyes."*

These well-known flowers have adorned the gardens, and been florists' favorites for many years. Their pleasing foliage, and brilliant bloom, well merit the estimation in which they are held. Leigh Hunt, the genial Essayist, says:—" Everything about the geranium is handsome, not excepting its name, which cannot be said of all flowers, though we get to love ugly words when associated with pleasing ideas. The word Geranium is soft and elegant; the meaning is poor, for it comes from a Greek word signifying a Crane, the fruit, or seed pod, resembling the form of a crane's bill. But what a reason for naming the flower! as if the fruit were anything in comparison, or any one cared about it. It would be far better to invent joyous and beautiful names for these images of joy and beauty."

Linnæus named the Geranium from *Geranos*, a crane, for the reason that Mr. Hunt gives. The plant is often confounded with the Pelargonium, which differs from it in size, shape and coloring of its flowers, and it is strictly exotic. It was named from *Pelargos*, a stork, on account of the resemblance of its capsules to the bill and head of that bird. They are placed in the same class of the Linnæan system as the Geranium (*Monadelphia*), but in the fourth order (*Heptandria*), while the other is in the sixth order (*Decandria*).

There has been a good deal of confusion with regard to the names of the two plants, and their numerous varieties, but the derivation of their titles settles the vexed question.

The careful and patient hybridization of the French, English and American florists have brought these flowers to a high standard of perfection.

The Double Geraniums.

Lemoine, the chief of the Geranium culturists, introduced the new double varieties, which have become a decided acquisition. They do not drop their leaves, like the single varieties, and their clusters of flowers are of an immense size. They are of all shades of scarlet and bright rosy pink; some have produced heads bearing from sixty to eighty perfect flowerets. They outrank all other kinds of Geraniums, and yearly their number increases. They flourish better if partially shaded from the intense heat of the noonday sun, and will bloom until the frost comes, in the greatest perfection.

No white variety has yet been introduced, but M. Lemoine will succeed in procuring one, if skill and patience can produce it.

Gloire de Nancy is a brilliant scarlet, much admired.

Marie Lemoine is a dwarf variety, of a bright rosy-pink hue, very elegant.

Emile Lemoine is of a cherry-carmine.

Gloire de Doubles is a novelty for 1871; of the richest cerise tint, with a distinct white center; far superior to the other varieties.

Crown Prince is of a dwarf habit, and of the brightest rose color.

The Zonale Geraniums.

But the double varieties are not the only ones which should claim our attention. Some of the new Zonale species are admirable in coloring, and of very free growth; their trusses of flowers are five to six inches in diameter; and they are found in all shades, from the most dazzling crimson and the brightest rose to the purest white.

The most desirable are:—

King of the Roses, a most brilliant scarlet, shaded to magenta.

Geant de Battailles, a dark, rich crimson.

Mrs. Keeler, of a rosy, peach-blossom hue.

Among the older varieties, and less costly, are:—

Christine, a lovely rosy-pink.

Gen. Grant, a dazzling scarlet, and decidedly the most profuse blower of the red varieties.

Incomparable has striped flowers, white on a clear salmon ground.

Maid of Kent, richest shade of pink.
Madame Werle, white, with a pink center.
Reine des Vierges, purest white.
Warrior, large clusters of the most intense scarlet; very superior.
Blue Bells, a rich shade of magenta pink, each blossom of immense size.
Coleshill, enormous scarlet truss, and blows freely.

Liliputian Zonales, or Tom Thumb Geraniums.

These comprise a dwarf section of this species, and grow from six to ten or twelve inches high; are very stocky, and their flowers equal in size and beauty of coloring those of larger growth. They are a very attractive plant, and make pretty borderings for beds or mounds of the taller kinds.
Baby Boy, scarlet, with white eye.
Little Dear, a delicate rose, spotted with white.
Little Gem, brilliant vermillion, with white center.
Christabel, very dwarf, rosy pink.
Cupid, a salmon color, with white eye.
Pretty Jemima, dazzling scarlet, white center.

Golden and Silver Tri-Color Geraniums.

These varieties are noticed under the head "Ornamental" Foliaged Plants; and the Ivy-Leaved Geraniums are embraced under the same heading.

The Sweet Scented Geraniums.

These plants are indispensable for bouquets and vases, their fragrance being agreeable to all lovers of flowers.

Formerly, the Rose and the Oak-Leaved were the only kinds commonly cultivated, but now there are a dozen varieties from which to make a selection, and all of them are desirable and beautiful, indeed, are quite essential, for there are few plants which afford such graceful backgrounds for borders or bouquets.

Denticulatum is a rose-scented variety, with finely cut foliage.
Lady Plymouth is also rose-scented, and its leaves are prettily margined with white.
Shrubland Pet is of dwarf growth, and very sweet scented.

Odoratissimum possesses a spicy apple perfume.

Graveolens is of a pleasant scent, with bright flowers.

All these plants will grow luxuriantly with but little care. Any one can raise Geraniums. They delight in a good, rich loam, with a mulch of manure; have a special fancy for "barn-yard coffee," or liquid manure. If watered with it, twice a week during the summer, will bloom profusely. If your plants are old, prune them closely, cutting the branches well in, and they will reward you for the sacrifice. If they are taken from pots, you should also prune the roots, cutting away all the largest roots to within five or six inches of the main stalk. After this vigorous pruning, the plants should not be exposed to the heat of the day, but must be shaded for a day or two, until they recover from their loss; but thus treated they will speedily put forth new roots, leaves and buds.

If the bed is shaded a little during the hottest part of the day, they will bloom the better.

To produce the largest clusters of flowers, the stalk above the buds should be pinched off, thus throwing all the strength of the plant into the formation of flowers.

A rich, light loam will grow Geraniums to perfection, and the soil fresh from the woods and pastures, if enriched with well-rotted cow manure, is the best that can be obtained. Plants delight in a virgin soil, and those who live in the country can provide themselves with it by lifting the sods from cow or sheep pastures, and taking the earth from under them.

If cuttings are desired from the Geraniums, they should be taken in July, from the healthiest plants, and planted in small pots filled with a compost of loam and sand, having one or two inches of the former on top of the pot. Insert the cutting firmly, and keep the sand sopping wet until it has rooted. When one or two leaves are developed, transplant it into a larger pot, with a compost of one-third rotted cow manure, one-third black loam, and one-third sand, and by November you will have vigorous plants for house culture. The large roots can be lifted from the ground before the frost blights their leaves, and after cutting away all the tender shoots and buds, and shaking the earth from their roots, hang them up in a dark, cool, dry, but frost-proof cellar, heads downward. In the Spring they can be brought to the light, the branches cut in, and though they will look shabby enough, yet, if planted in boxes in a warm kitchen, they will put forth leaves and vegetate rapidly, and can then be transplanted into the borders. The tender branches and buds should be cut off, else they will continue for awhile to grow in the cellar, and thus lose their lives.

Cuttings can be started in the open borders, but they are not as sure to live. It is no more trouble to grow a Geranium than a cabbage, yet one is far more desirable than the other, unless hunger is at the door.

Geraniums are never attacked by the aphis, or red spider, and this is a great attribute; one is not forced to fight for their lives.

The Pelargonium.

The flowers of this plant are much sought after on account of their perfect coloring and blotches. There are all shades of scarlet, crimson, pink, purple and white; the lower leaves, and frequently the upper, are veined and blotched with the darkest crimson, purple and red, beautifully veined with the lighter shades. The leaves of the plant are more pleasantly perfumed than those of the Geranium, and have no zonale, or horse-shoe markings, but are of a rich, vivid green. No description can convey any idea of the beauty of the flowers. They bloom in border or bed all the summer, and are to be had in hundreds of varieties. They are propagated both from cuttings and seeds, and the "novelties" are produced by careful hybridization. They require a light, sandy loam, well enriched with cow manure, and if they are not plentifully supplied with water, their buds will wither away. They need more sunlight than the Geranium to bloom in perfection. Some of them are tall in growth, and produce a good effect planted singly on the lawn. They are the most showy-flowered of all the bedding-out plants, excepting the Scarlet Salvia, and their varied tints and exquisite colors make them very desirable in the smallest garden.

Their habit is not always compact, but they can be cut and trimmed to a fine shape, and the older plants require such treatment to bloom well, the second year.

Among the many varieties offered for our selection, the most desirable ones are:—

Gen. Taylor, of a rich crimson, blotched with the darkest tint of red.
Niagara, white, striped and blotched with crimson.
Competitor, black, edged with rose.

Emperor of Pelargonium, very large flower of snowy whiteness, spotted with violet, tinged with rose; petals finely fringed.

Eligible, a pink crimson, with white edges, and violet blotches and veins.

Dr. Andre, pink and white, petals fringed.

Cloth of Silver, petals of silvery whiteness, blotched with delicate rose.

Crimson King, a rich crimson, beautifully veined and blotched.

Princess Hortense, orange-salmon, edged with pink.

Eclipse, clear white petals, marked with maroon.

Belle of Paris, rich violet crimson, upper petals spotted; an immense cluster of flowers.

CHAPTER VI.

BEDDING-OUT PLANTS, PANSIES, VERBENAS, HELIOTROPES, FEVERFEWS, ETC.

"Your voiceless lips, O flowers, are living preachers!
Each cup a pulpit, every leaf a book!
Supplying to my fancy numerous teachers
From loneliest nook."

The varieties of plants called by florists bedding-out plants, are very popular—and deservedly so. Their flowers present a brilliant mess of coloring all the summer, and their hues are richer than those of most other flowers.

Pansies are great favorites—they will grow in shady nooks where no other flower can bloom—and their flowers continue from the earliest spring until the latest autumn. Various and familiar are the names by which the Pansy has been known for centuries.

Gerard, who wrote a long description of it, says it was known as Love-in-idleness, Jump-up-and-kiss-me, Three-faces-under-a-hood, Heart's-ease, and Pansy. The Italians named it *Nola farfalla* (Violet Butterfly).

Lady Mary Bennet of England, afterwards Lady Monck, first introduced the Pansy to the attention of the florists. Early in the present century, she planted all the varieties of the Heart's-ease which she could procure, and with the skillful aid of her gardener, new varieties were produced from seed.

About 1813, the well-known florist, Mr. Lee, of Vineyard Nursery, at Hammersmith, saw Lady Mary's collection, and immediately perceived the profit that would accrue from the cultivation of this flower. His skill and patience were rewarded by the production of still more beautiful varieties. Other nurserymen followed his example, and in a few years the unpretending Heart's-ease took its place as a florist's flower of no small pretensions. The French name *Pensées* was the origin of the English word Pansy.

Milton alludes to it as the "pansy freak'd with jet" amongst those "vernal flowers," whose "quaint enamel'd eyes a sad embroidery wear." Another writer says:—

> "Are not Pansies emblems meet for thought?
> The pure, the chequered—gay and deep by turns;
> A line for every mood the bright things wear,
> In their soft, velvety coats."

One must not suppose that rich soil or careful culture have wrought such wonderful changes in the Pansey. This is only the first step in the march of improvement.

The seeds of the finest flowers were carefully preserved, and the finest of the young seedlings were selected for seed. Hybrids were also obtained by fertilizing the stigma of one rarely colored flower, with the pollen of another of a larger variety. These hybrids generally possess in a great degree the peculiar qualities of each parent, and retain their peculiar markings.

Innumerable are the varieties now cultivated; there are upwards of a thousand named kinds catalogued by the English nurserymen.

Mrs. Loudon says in her book upon "Floriculture," that "the varieties of forms and colors which appear in the plants raised from seed are so great that few floricultural pursuits can be more interesting than to sow a bed of Pansies, and watch when they flower for the varieties most desirable to perpetuate."

By judicious management, a successive bloom can be retained for eight months in the year, and even a slight attention to their needs is rewarded by a profusion of beautiful flowers. There is no bedding-out plant which gives a more liberal supply of flowers—from the earliest spring to the latest autumn.

Plants from seed blossom finely the first year, and give much larger flowers when the plant is small, for as it increases in size, the blooms though abundant are smaller and inferior in coloring.

A constant succession of flowering plants should be brought forward during the spring and summer months, and the plants kept young and vigorous. This is often done by cuttings as well as seedlings. They can be grown more rapidly, and are certain to produce fine flowers.

The cuttings should be taken from the points of the shoots, and cut about three inches long, and immediately below a joint. Strip off the lower leaves, and plant them in sand, pressing the soil closely around the stem. If planted on the north side of a fence or hedge in a sheltered location, with an inch of sand covering the cuttings, they will strike rapidly. If in pots, they should be covered with glass. In about six weeks they will be well rooted, and fit to transplant into the flowering beds, or into pots for window gardening.

Pansies are often layered, by pegging down the young shoots with a hair pin, and covering all but an inch or two of the point with fine sand.

An incision can be made at the joint, as is done in layering roses, but frequently they will make root equally as well without using the knife.

When rooted, which can be told by the growth of new leaves—separate from the old plant, and either plant out in borders or in pots.

They can also be increased by dividing the old roots, and the divisions will soon make fine plants.

Seed can be sown early in the season, in a hot-bed—following directions given for planting seed, in Chapter II, and when the fourth or fifth leaves are formed, the plants can be put into the borders, and planted a foot apart each way to allow them room to grow.

Pansies are very gross feeders, delighting in the richest soil, with plenty of liquid manure. If large blossoms are desired, the soil must be of the richest description.

The best compost for them is one-third leaf mould, one-third thoroughly decayed barn-yard manure, and one-third light loam. In this soil they will blossom most gorgeously. The location should be on the northwest side of the house, and shaded from the noonday sun. They will not grow to advantage in either light, sandy soil, or much sunlight, but require moisture and shade, and copious waterings to produce perfect flowers. They are also great deteriorators of the soil, and will soon run out unless it is renewed. New beds do much better than old ones. After they have blossomed freely until July, cut down the branches several inches, mulch with well-rotted cow manure, and by September they will be in a blaze of glory.

If the amateur florist desires to sow the seed from some especially rare flowers, they should be carefully tied up, and no other flower be allowed to go to seed on the same plant.

The seed may be sown in spring, summer or autumn; in the two former seasons it can be planted in the open ground; in the latter in pots, so that the tender seedlings can be protected from the damp. Pansies are hardy perennials, but will wither away if water settles on the bed. They do not like either the wintry ice, or the excessive heat of summer.

Violets, Sweet Violets.

These flowers cannot compare with their beauteous sisters—the Pansies —in size or colorings; they cannot boast such varied blotchings and veinings, but they possess a higher attribute in their rarely delicious odor—their perfume is unsurpassed by that of any other flower. They are always in demand, and are very easily raised. With slight protection they will live in the coldest climate, and before the Snow-drop hangs its pearly bell, they will be in full bloom.

The Viola odorissima is the English variety most extensively cultivated. Several new varieties have been introduced; among them the double blue Neapolitan is the most popular. The King of Violets has a very large flower, and is much cultivated for window gardens. The Czar is a fine variety; and the Schœnbrun is a single variety, very sweet. There are white varieties, that are also much used by florists, but the blues are the greatest favorites.

The Violet is the emblematic flower of the Bonapartes, as the Lily is of the Bourbons. Dame Rumor tells us that Eugenie expressed her willingness to accept the offer of becoming Louis Napoleon's wife by dressing in an exquisite violet toilet—violets in her hair, about her dress, and a bouquet of them in her hand, which were perfectly significant to the wooer. The great Napoleon selected it as his flower, through Josephine's requesting it as a birthday gift.

He cultivated them in large quantities in his garden at St. Helena, and they were planted over the grave of Josephine, and when he was buried, his coffin was covered with the flowers he loved so well.

Louis Napoleon is said to have made himself acquainted with those who were friendly to his interests, while carefully feeling his way to the throne, by a cautious display of violets. Sweet violets!

The Heliotrope.

Heliotropes fill an important place among "bedding-out" plants, giving us a plentiful supply of flowers from June to October. They are desirable for their fragrance, as well as for their profusion of flowers. They were introduced into England from Peru in 1757, and the cottagers called it "Cherry Pie," from a fancied resemblance in its fragrance to the odor of that esteemed dish. It has also been called the "Vanilla Plant." The flower first introduced was of a light lavender shade, and for many years no change of color was effected, but now it is offered from the darkest purple to the faintest shade of lavender.

They make very fine standards, trained from a single stem, from one to four feet high, with a head of several feet in diameter.

The older the plant, the more profuse are its clusters of fragrant flowers. A cutting in the first year will grow very rank, but if cut back and pruned into one stem, it becomes woody, and will make a fine shrub. In California, they bloom as plentifully at Christmas as at Fourth of July, and it is not uncommon to see large trellises and walls covered with its branches and exquisite flowers—perfect bouquets of beauty, being always covered with flowers. The main stems of the plant are trained to the wall, and the branches droop gracefully. Any kind of turfy loam will grow it perfectly. It is propagated from cuttings with great ease.

Of the very dark varieties, Etoile de Marseilles ranks first; flowers of a deep violet with white center.

Duc de Lavendry is of a rich blush, with a dark eye.
Incomparable is of a lovely bluish-lilac.
Garibaldi is nearly white.
Leopold 1st, of a deep violet blue.
Madame Facilon, a clear violet tint.
Malulatie is of the most delicate lilac.

Verbenas.

Among all the variety of "bedding-out" plants, which contribute to the gay and lively appearance of a garden, the Verbena is the most generally cultivated, and claims the first rank among brilliant flowers. Some of its varieties are sweet scented, but most of them depend for their merit upon their showy, gorgeous coloring, and their wonderful profusion of blossoms, which render them of the greatest value. There have been some splendid, new varieties introduced in the few past years, whose wondrous stripes and eyes are not approached by any of the older sorts. They are selected from many thousand seedlings, and are both rich and rare.

But any one can raise new varieties from seed, and good culture will produce magnificent blooms. Seedlings will seed much more plentifully than flowers from cuttings, and the older the cutting the less seed it will give.

Verbenas do not sprout readily from seed; they are encased in a horny substance, and should be soaked in warm water for twenty-four hours, and then planted in a light sandy loam, with a good bottom heat. Thus treated they will germinate, and when the fourth leaf is formed, should be potted into thumb pots in sandy loam.

Verbenas are natives of Brazil, and love the hot sun and sand. If the bed in which they are planted is covered two or three inches deep with common sand, they will bloom most perfectly.

I once raised seventy verbenas from seed, and planted them in a very sandy soil. Such growth I never witnessed—they were magnificent! As the plant sends out its first shoots, they should be pegged down with hair-pins, and thus coaxed to grow. When watered they desire a copious supply, and the suds from washing-day are very beneficial to them. Guano is also a good manure for them; dig an iron spoonful around each plant, not touching the stems. The green lice, or *aphis*, are their plague in pot culture, but they are destroyed by smoking them with tobacco. Put the plants together, and throw some tobacco on hot coals in a pot saucer; cover the whole with a wash tub, and let them smoke for ten or fifteen minutes, and the lice can be swept up and burned. Place the coals as far as possible from the plants, under the tubs, so as not to injure them with their heat.

If plants are well showered, no lice will appear—they do not love moisture.

If cuttings are desired for winter bloom, they should be taken off in August, so as to become well rooted. It never pays to take up old plants for winter blooming.

Among the new Verbenas for 1871, are:—
Annie, white, crimson striped.
Black Bedder, richest maroon.
Conspicua, ruby-scarlet, white eye.

Cupid, very large, white, tinted with pink.
Distinction, solferino, dark eye.
Gazelle, deep blue, clear white eye.
Iona, large scarlet, yellow eye.
Muriel, ruby-pink, white eye.
Punctata, spotted and striped with carmine.
Rising Sun, crimson, white eye.
Sensation, waxy white, carmine eye.
Snow Storm, pure white, large and fine.
Spot, carmine, white eye.
Tricolor, carmine, crimson and orange.
Unique, white, carmine spot.

All these varieties originated with Peter Henderson, the Prince of American Floriculture, and are sure to be true to description. Any one can raise a Verbena, and no garden can be complete without some of the hundreds of varieties offered by all florists.

Salvias.

These plants are the most gorgeous of all the fall-flowering plants; they grow from four to five feet high; and the small plant, you purchase in the spring of the florist, will become by September a beautiful, symmetrical bush, covered with tassels of the brightest scarlet flowers. They are unequaled for planting in masses, but are very tender, the first frost rendering them a blackened mass.

Salvia splendens variegata is a novelty possessing finely variegated foliage, with flowers as brilliant as the common kind. The roots can be hung up in the cellar in the winter—like the Geraniums.

Salvia patens is of a deep blue color, of the most perfect shade. It has a tuberous root, which can be kept like a Dahlia through the winter, in sand.

The Ageratum.

These plants are excellent for beds and borders, on account of their constant bloom. Their flowers are of light porcelain blue, in large clusters.

Ageratum Mexicanum is of a light blue.

A, variegatum has leaves variegated with yellow, shading with crimson.

A, Tom Thumb variety, growing from six to eight inches, is desirable for ribbon gardening; contrasting beautifully with dark crimson leaves.

Carnations, Calceolarias, Gazanias, Feverfews, Lobelias, Lantanas, Neirembergias, Vincas, etc., etc., are all desirable for bedding-out plants, and can all be raised from cuttings or seeds, but the former is the surest mode of propagation.

How to Grow Cuttings of Geraniums, Verbenas, etc., etc.

To prepare pots for raising cuttings, fill them two-thirds full, with rich loam, dark and porous, not clayey and heavy; then pour on an inch or two of yellow sand. Wet this thoroughly, and place the cuttings close to the edge of the pot; the contact of the pottery promotes the growth of the cutting. Cuttings should be taken from the young and newly-formed wood of the plant; but the lower extremity of it should not be too young and soft, else it will absorb too much moisture and decay; neither should it be too old and hard, for then it will not imbibe moisture enough to enable it to throw out roots. Therefore, cuttings should be taken off at the junction of the old and new wood, so that these extremes will be avoided. They should be cut off just below a joint or bud, as the roots start from that point; and, if a bud is not left at the base, it is liable to decay; the cut should be made smooth across the stem, taking care not to bruise the bark, or leave it jagged. Most of the hardy, wooded shrubs and plants are easily propagated by cuttings planted in the open air; but the tender, watery-stemmed plants like Verbenas, Heliotropes, Fuchsias, etc., should be covered with a hand glass, or raised in a hot-bed. A certain amount of heat, moisture and shade is required to enable cuttings to strike roots. Shade is needful, because an exposure to the sun or strong light evaporates the little moisture contained in the cuttings, and causes them to wither away.

So, for three days, or until the cutting becomes wonted to its location, shade from exclusive sunlight.

Peter Henderson recommends saucer propagation.

Take a common saucer or shallow dish, fill it with wet sand and insert the cuttings, pressing the sand close about them. Keep it sopping wet; if allowed to dry it will check the growth; when the old leaves have dropped, and new ones appear at the point of the cutting, roots have formed; and the plant may be carefully potted in light, sandy loam shaded for a day, and then have all the sunshine it desires, if it has also sufficient water, but you must not let it dry up.

Cuttings of many plants can be readily started in water; and, in the early spring, if you have not a green-house or hot-bed, it is the safest plan.

Fill small bottles or vials, with warmish water, remove the lower leaves of the cuttings (be sure to have a bud at the base), and put them in the water; hang up the vial to the window sash, tying a string about the mouth, for this purpose. If cotton wool is put around the mouth of the vial, it will prevent the evaporation of the water, and make the roots sprout more quickly by keeping up a more even temperature. Oleanders can be rooted in this manner; also Heliotropes, Verbenas, Roses, Fuchsias, and all kinds bedding-out plants.

The process is so simple that a mere child can succeed with it. As soon as the roots are an inch long, the cutting should be transplanted, taking care to spread out the tiny rootlets as they grow in the water.

Some fill up the bottle with rich earth, let it dry off for two or three days and then break the glass, and pot or plant out the cutting without disturbing its roots in the least degree. This is the most certain way of obtaining plants from cuttings.

CHAPTER VII.

THE FUCHSIA.

"Thou graceful flower, on graceful stem,
Of Flora's gifts a fav'rite gem !
From tropic fields thou cam'st to cheer
The natives of a climate drear;
And grateful for our fostering care,
Has learn'd the wintry blast to bear."

Although Fuchsias, on their first introduction into England, seventy-three or four years ago, were treated as stove plants; they scarcely come under the head of Window Gardening, as many of the species live in sheltered gardens throughout the year, both in England and in this country. In California, they bloom for twelve months in the year, and grow into large bushes, perfectly covered with brilliant flowers. Their light and graceful appearance renders them desirable in the smallest garden. Their gorgeous pendant flowers, with petals of the richest scarlet dye, shading down to the palest pink, or the purest white, with corollas of glowing purple, scarlet, pink or white, produce a most attractive whole, and entitle them to a chapter by themselves, for they are the chief among "bedding-out" plants.

To their glorious beauty, Fuchsias add three other desirable requisites: their free growth, their general hardiness, and the ease with which they are propagated.

In bedding them out, a moist, shady position is the most suitable; our noonday sun scorches the tender buds, and causes them to fall. Their native home is in Brazil, where Darwin saw large thickets of them, and they choose moist locations in the woods. In rich, loamy soil, well mixed with leaf mould and rotted cow manure, the growth of a young cutting is very rapid, and will make a large plant by the autumn. When it has commenced to grow, don't check it by neglect, but during the Summer months water twice a day with tepid water, and, if possible, give it liquid manure water, either from the barn-yard, or by dissolving one table-spoonful of guano in one gallon of warm water; water with this twice a week, and its growth will astonish you. Fuchsias are as gross feeders as the Pansy, and luxuriate in the richest soil; thus treated, some kinds will send out shoots from four to five feet in length in six or eight months.

They show to great advantage when trained as standards; to do this, the side shoots of a young plant must be nipped off, and the stem trained up a straight stick. When the plant grows high enough for your purpose, let the side shoots branch out, and you can grow a fine tree. They can also be trained to walls, or planted in masses in beds. If the young plant does not branch out, pinch off the terminal shoot, and side branches will appear, and the most central shoot can be trained up for a leader. If plants are set near the cooling spray of a fountain, they thrive well, but must not be so near as to keep their roots constantly wet.

Culture.

Many gardeners prefer to have new plants every season, but if old ones are judiciously cared for, they will produce a finer effect, and bloom more profusely. Large plants can be kept in frost-proof, dry cellars during the winter, either in pots or in boxes; or they can be pulled up by the roots, the soil shaken from them, and packed in layers in sand which is thoroughly dry, first cutting off all the tender shoots. In March or April they can be brought to the light, and planted in good, rich soil, pruning not only the top, but the roots. In cutting the top back, have an eye to its shape, and prune accordingly.

Some of the Fuchsias are of much taller growth than others. Speciosa will grow six to eight feet in height; Pride of England is a small bush compared to it; while Souvenir de Cheswick will readily train into a fine standard.

Plants must be allowed to follow their natural habits in some respects.

To Grow Cuttings.

Fuchsias will strike root as rapidly as Geraniums. Take the cuttings either in February, March or April, from three to four inches long

Plant in clear sand, keep "sopping wet," and in three weeks they will be well rooted. Pot in three-inch pots, in the richest of soil, with a little sand to keep it mellow; let them grow until the pot is well filled with roots, which will be in three or four weeks, then repot in six to eight inch pots, if designed to grow in them; but if raised to bed out, plant in five-inch pots, and when all fear of frost is passed, plant in the open borders.

Be sure not to let the summer heat kill your plants. They will grow well under trees, if the branches are fifteen feet or more from the ground, so that the air can circulate freely. These plants are liable to lose their leaves and buds if the soil is not rich enough to their taste, and red spiders often infest them, ruining their growth. For the poverty of the soil, either repot entirely, or give a top dressing of manure; for the spiders, sprinkle daily, and they may be driven off—they do not love water; but if this remedy fails, dip the whole plant into water quite warm to the hand. A dusting of sulphur will kill them, but it often kills the leaves also.

I was much troubled with spiders last season, on fine plants of Marksman and Carl Halt. I dusted them over with "Grafton Mineral Fertilizer," and destroyed every one. I scattered the same powder over the soil, digging in a teaspoonful to each pot (size eight inches), and in September the plants were in a blaze of glory, the admiration of every passer-by.

The Double Flowering Fuchsias.

By careful culture from seed, these brilliant varieties were produced, and are unsurpassed for beauty and elegance by any plant in the floral world. Studded all over with their bright wealth of jewels, they far outshine their single brethren.

Elm City held front rank for some years, but Marksman far surpasses it now, and Warrior is said to eclipse all others. It has a scarlet tube and sepals, with a rich violet-purple corolla, and possesses a vigorous habit. So numerous are the varieties of these charming flowers, that one can hardly make a selection, when all are so desirable, but from the lists of English and American florists I cull the following, to add to those above mentioned:—

Select List of Double Fuchsias.

Tower of London, scarlet sepals, violet-blue corolla.
Surpasse V. de Puebla, scarlet sepals, double white corolla.

Monstrosa, bright rose sepals, double white corolla.
Norfolk Giant, crimson sepals, violet corolla.
Nonpareil, two corollas, the stamens forming a second corolla of a purplish blue; very elegant.
E. G. Henderson, scarlet sepals, rich violet corolla.
Wilhelm Pfitzer, rosy-carmine sepals, corolla lavender-blue.
Symbol, crimson tube and sepals, creamy-white corolla.
Emperor of the Fuchsias, sepals crimson, white corolla.
Grand Duke, crimson, violet-purple corolla.
Picturata, scarlet sepals, double white corolla.
Snowdrop, sepals bright scarlet, semi-double white corolla.

Select List of Single Fuchsias.

Charming, violet corolla, crimson sepals, immense clusters.
Annie, tube and sepals white, corolla deep pink.
Arabella, white sepals, corolla richest pink; earliest variety.
Jules Calot, sepals of an orange red, orange-crimson corolla.
Lustre, vermillion corolla, waxy-white sepals; early.
Prince Imperial, scarlet sepals, large violet corolla.
Father Ignatius, carmine sepals, blue corolla, bell shaped.
Fairest of the Fair, violet-rose corolla, white tube and sepals.
Land of Plenty, rich red sepals, violet-black corolla.
Marginata, white sepals, pink corolla, shaded to bright rose color.
Rose of Castile, violet corolla, sepals white.
Souvenir de Cheswick, rosy-crimson sepals, violet corolla.
Striped Unique, purple corolla, striped with scarlet.
Tagliona, white reflexed sepals, dark violet corolla.
Wave of Life, violet-blue corolla, scarlet sepals, gold tinted foliage.
Weeping Beauty, scarlet sepals, large blue corolla.

The Golden Leaved Fuchsias.

Of this variety there have been but two specimens, Cloth of Gold and Golden Fleece, until the importation of 1871, when several more were added to the list which have attracted much attention in England for their beautiful foliage and graceful habit.

Crown of Jewels, leaves clear yellow, tipped with rich red crimson, ornamental at all seasons.
Golden Mantle, golden yellow leaves, flowers coral red.

Golden Treasure, very attractive, gold colored leaves tinted with bronze.

Orange Boven, the smallest variety grown; golden leaves tipped with bronze.

The Winter Flowering Fuchsias.

These are few in number—only two varieties, which are sure to bloom from December to May.

Speciosa is well known; it produces flowers two inches in length, tubes and sepals are a waxen peach-blossom color, with crimson corolla.

Serratifolia is an equally valuable variety; the flowers are distinct from any other Fuchsia. The tube of the flower is crimson, the tips of the sepals shading to green, corolla light crimson, with white stamens. Both these plants are extensively cultivated, and, if well fed, will bloom profusely when flowers are a rarity.

CHAPTER VIII.

CULTIVATION OF THE ROSE.

> "Nymphs who haunt th' embowering shades,
> Poesy's enchanting maids,
> Woo thee, Rose! Thy charms inspire
> All the raptures of the lyre;
> Cull we straight the inviting Rose,
> Shielded by the thorn it grows;
> Cull the Rose! what boots the smart?
> Countless sweets regale the heart."

Thus sang Anacreon, the Greek poet, hundreds of years ago, in praise of the Queen of Flowers, which was used to decorate the temple and the palace—the solemn rites of religion, and the festal gayety of the banquet.

France excels all other nations in the production of new varieties of this lovely flower. The Empress Josephine collected every variety then cultivated, for a rosary at Malmaison; and, under her patronage, the culture of roses became speedily the fashion. The skill and patience of the florists produced more beautiful varieties, under the stimulus thus given to their trade; and they have continued to give us yearly many rich and rare roses; but have not yet succeeded in producing a blue rose. The English florists are but little behind the French, in their attention to this charming flower; and our own nurserymen yearly produce many beautiful varieties.

Thousands of named sorts are offered to us; and it is very hard to make a selection when all possess so much merit. It is usually best, in purchasing plants, to leave the selection to the florist, merely stating the climate, and soil in which they will grow.

It is also best to grow roses on their roots, unless "standards" are desired, for the old roots will throw up strong suckers, and thus assert their rights to the detriment of their nursling; unless these are constantly watched for, and cut off, they will destroy the graft.

The varieties of the rose have increased with such rapidity in the last twelve years, and they have produced so many new *races*, that it is scarcely possible for the most skillful botanist to refer each variety to its proper parent species. There are Hybrid Perpetuals, Bourbons, Bengal, Chinese or Daily Rose; Tea-scented, Noisette, Perpetual Moss, Annual Moss, Prairie Rose as climbers; Scotch, Damask and all the old varieties of Garden Roses.

From the thousands of names offered in the catalogues, lists of those most desirable will be given; but, of course, every one has his own pet fancies.

There is no plant which requires a richer soil or better repays the cultivator for attending to its wants; when grown in a congenial soil its blossoms are perfect.

The best soil is fresh loam enriched with well-rotted cow manure, with a little sand. If a top dressing of this compost is given every spring before the buds start, the branches will make fine growth.

The finest clusters of flowers are always produced on new wood, and close pruning will cause more new wood to grow, and ensure you a more splendid show of flowers. Use the knife freely, though it does make you ache to do so; cut all the old growth out, and prune in last year's branches a little; thus pruned, the roots will throw up new shoots, from whence will come the finest roses of the garden.

As soon as the plants have done flowering, thin out the weak shoots, and even some of the stronger ones, if they are too crowded; each shoot left, should be exposed on every side to air and sun. The summer flowering kinds thus treated will continue their growth from the main shoots, and bloom much finer another year; while the autumnal flowers push forth their buds the entire length of the stalk, and the second flowering is perfected.

The roses are improved in both varieties; for shoots grown at that period of the year invariably produce the finest flowers.

It has been recommended by some writers, to destroy the first bloom of those roses which bloom twice in the season; because there is an abundance of roses in June, and by so doing a finer bloom is obtained in the autumn. Too many roses! Has any one ever witnessed such a season? Let them bloom when they will, and cut off the stems as soon as the leaves fall; then remove the soil to the depth of three or four inches, and spread over it, almost close to the stem, a spadeful of cow manure well decayed; throw back the soil that was removed, and, if the weather is hot and dry, water occasionally, and you will have a vigorous growth and a profuse flowering.

The flower stalk should always be cut off; it exhausts the plant to form seeds, and consumes the strength which should go to forming new shoots. When roses are planted in lawns, they should have no sods near the roots; for the grass will absorb all the moisture, and also prevent the air from reaching the soil.

The best time to plant hardy roses is in October or November, according to the climate.

Spring months are better for planting half-hardy and tender roses, as their roots will not get started before winter sets in. Of course, in the mild climates of the Southern States, they can also be planted in the late autumn. When first set out they should be mulched with coarse manure, and watered occasionally, if the weather is warm and dry.

Cuttings of Roses.

Roses are propagated chiefly by cuttings, layers and buds. Cuttings of the hardy kind of roses, will strike easily in July and August. Hybrid Perpetual, Chinese and Bourbon, with all the other kinds will grow readily, if the cutting has, what gardeners term, a heel; that is, cut off close to the old wood. Three, four or even six eyes can be left above ground.

Plant them as recommended in chapter six; in wet sand. A dozen cuttings can be set an inch apart, close to the pot; and the sand should not be allowed to dry at all. If covered with a "*cloche*," or hand-glass, a moist temperature will be kept up, and, in two or three weeks, they will commence to grow.

Layering Roses.

Roses grown as dwarfs or bushes are the kind that will layer advantageously. Loosen the soil about the plant, then choose a good shoot, strip off a few leaves from six inches to two feet from the point of the shoot; insert a sharp knife just behind an eye, on the upper side of the shoot, and pass it carefully upwards cutting about half through the stem, and from an inch to two inches in length. Open the soil, bend down the shoots and press it in; peg it down with a hair pin or a bit of wood, two or three inches beneath the soil, and cover it firmly. Each layer should be tied to a stake to prevent the wind from disturbing the roots.

June, July and August are the best months for layering. If the weather is dry and hot, water frequently. Don't let the layers dry up; about October or November they will be large enough to take away. Cut them off within two inches of the root, and transplant them wherever they are desired. In the spring prune the stem down to three or four eyes, and they will bloom finely.

The Chinese method of layering is often more successful than any other.

At the end of July or beginning of August, they select a strong shoot of the same year's growth, tongue it, as described above, and put in a small stone to keep the slit open, and bind a handful of fresh green moss around the tongue. This must be kept constantly wet, and the tiny roots will shoot forth into the moss so rapidly, that in five or six weeks the layer can be removed from the parent stalk. The roots can be planted without disturbing the moss, and fine plants are thus procured.

Budding Roses.

Budding roses is a very simple process, and an old razor can do duty for a budding knife, and the handle of an old toothbrush, if scraped down smooth, will answer for a wedge.

The latter part of June to the middle of August, is the best season for budding; or, when the bark of the stalk can be easily raised from the wood, this is a sure sign that one can bud with success.

Take a smooth part of the stem at the height you desire, and on the side least exposed to the sun; with the razor make a horizontal cut across the bark through to the wood, but not in to it; from the center of this cross-cut make one straight down the stem, an inch or more in length; these two cuts should be in the form of a **T**.

Now prepare the bud, or shield, as it is termed. Slice it off from the rose you desire to bud from at one cut, and the shoot must be cut off close to the main stalk; then the bud is sliced off, with a portion of the old wood adhering to it; most of this should be picked out, but a little at the back of the bud is essential to life; if you make a hole through its bark throw it away, it will not grow.

Now, with the thin edge of the toothbrush handle, turn back the stem on each side of the straight cut, and insert the bud close to the wood, and fit it accurately and firmly to the cross-cut in the turned-back bark; on this close contact of the two barks will depend the success of your operation.

Lay the turned-back bark closely over the bud, or shield, and with woolen yarn, or a bit of bass-wood, bind it down, leaving the point of the bud clear.

Common adhesive plaster is said to be better for this purpose than either yarn or bass. A handful of damp moss should be tied around the whole, leaving the tiny point of the bud exposed to the air.

In six weeks at the farthest these ties can be removed.

All other shoots on that stem should be cut off, so as to throw the strength of the plant into the support of the new comer.

By budding you may produce several kinds of roses upon the same plant. Take a common wild rose, cut down all its suckers, and trim in its branches, and bud with white, pink, crimson and yellow roses.

As soon as the buds commence to grow, cut off all the wild shoots, and you will have a beautiful show of flowers.

Variegated shrubs can be budded in this manner upon the plain green stocks. Grafting roses is not so popular as formerly; but the operation is easily performed. Any one who can graft a tree, can graft a rose. The stock to be grafted should be more forward than the scion, and the operation should be performed when the sap is rising. April or May are the best months.

The most important points in a good rose are, that its "constitution should be hardy, and vigorous, with a robust habit of growth, good foliage and profuse bloom. The flower should be fine in form, large in size, decided in color. The form of the flower, whether it be globular, cupped, or widely expanded, should be symmetrical; the petals even and regular in their arrangement, full but not too crowded; the outer range broad and firmly set, rendering the flower more lasting. In texture they should be firm and thick, not thin and flimsy. Fragrance, and a firm upright stem are desirable points. A green or yellow center to a flower when fully open, is a great fault. There is no kind of shrub in existence so well adapted to take various forms as the rose. It can be used as a dwarf to fill the smallest beds; as a shrub to plant among evergreens; and as a tall standard to form avenues of roses on each side of a walk.

It can be planted in groups with a climber in the center, half standards around it, and dwarfs for an edging; again, as climbers to adorn a villa or a cottage, also to cover bare walls and trellises. Yet none of these forms will show off its beauty and elegance as effectually as training it to a pillar.

Pillar Roses.

Iron rods with arches of the same material, or small chains hung loosely from pillar to pillar so as to form festoons, will produce a charming effect, making a lovely bower.

The pillars can be made either of a single upright post, or four rods can be set at about nine inches distant from each other, thus forming a square pillar, fastened with interlacings of strong copper wire.

The rose can be planted in the center, and the branches trained to each corner rod, the small shoots twined between them. Bring all the shoots to the outside, and do not let any twine round the rods, but tie them to each with strings; and whenever they require painting, which is needful to protect the iron from rusting, or, if the plants are tender, and need protection, they are easily loosened from their support. Poles of oak, ash or pine can supply the places of the iron rods; and, by fixing them firmly into the ground in a triangular shape, three feet apart at the base, and fastening the tops together with strong copper wire, a pyramid of different colors can be formed, by planting three different roses at the foot of the poles, and training them so that the various hues will be seen.

Weeping Roses.

These form beautiful objects when planted singly on lawns. Roses of a pendulous habit must be used, such as the Aryshire and Evergreen. Bud them on stocks four feet or upwards in height; the main shoots, after the second year, should not be shortened until they touch the ground; prune only the side branches, and the flowers will be produced from all along the branches from the head to the ground.

When they attain their full size a hoop shall be attached to prevent the branches from blowing about in the wind.

Slugs on Rose Bushes.

For several years past these pests have ruined the glory of the "Queen of Flowers," and turned her beauty into deformity, changing the ornaments of the garden with unsightly bushes, sparsely covered with skeleton leaves.

Before the buds are formed, minute white spots appear on the under surface of the leaves; these change rapidly into horrid green worms which devour all the green part of the leaves, and also the buds and flowers. If taken in season they can be destroyed. I used "Grafton Mineral Fertilizer" with great effect last season, keeping the foliage of a tall pink Moss Rose entirely free from their ravages; while directly across the path, a yellow Harrison was left to them, and was utterly ruined.

The powder is inodorous; can be scattered over the leaves before the dew is dried off, and will drive them away. I made the first application in May, a second one early in June, and a third after the roses had fled. Not a green worm was seen on the leaves. The foliage was perfect.

Powdered lime, if scattered over the leaves while wet with dew, will also keep them off.

A few years ago I saw a most beautiful rose garden at Plattsburgh, N. Y., not a slug had touched the leaves, and it was early in July. The lady owner told me that the bushes were syringed with ten gallons of warm water, in which one pint of soft soap, and one pint of common fine salt had been dissolved. This mixture killed them all. It was applied in May, and again in June.

Other preparations are used; white hellebore, sprinkled on through a dredging box, and flour of sulphur, similarly applied, are found efficacious. There are two crops of the slugs; the first comes in May, and when the worms are fully developed they burrow in the ground, and lie in a chrysalis state until August, when they appear with wings, and lay a crop of eggs for the ensuing summer. If the first crop are not entirely destroyed, it is well to repeat the application in August, so as to diminish the supply for the next season.

The following comprises a good collection of Hybrid Perpetuals:—

Achille Gonaud, bright carmine.

Alex. Bachmeteff, deep, brilliant rose, large and fine.

Baron Prevost, rich rose color.

Cardinal Patrizzi, dark, velvety crimson.

Comte Litta, velvety purple.
Caroline de Sansal, pale flesh color.
Eugene Appert, scarlet crimson.
Gen. Jacqueminot, brilliant red, very large.
John Hopper, rosy-crimson, extra.
Jules Margottin, carmine, shaded to purple.
La Reine, clear rose, large cupped, superb.
Lady Emily Peel, white, edged with rose.
Mad'lle Bonnaire, pure white, tinged with rose at the center.
Mad. Freeman, white, with yellowish shade.
Pœonia, deep brilliant crimson.
Reine des Violets, reddish violet.
Victor Verdier, large, full carmine, one of the best.

Bourbon Roses.

Archduke Charles, rosy crimson.
Bourbon Queen, rich blush.
Blanche Lafitte, pale flesh color, beautiful.
Duchesse Furringe, white.
Empress Eugene, deep rose.
Jupiter, dark purple.
Hermosa Pink, a profuse bloomer, with lovely buds.
Malmaison, blush, large and fine.
Omar Pasha, deep carmine.
Paxton, bright rose, crimson shaded.
Sombreuil, white.

Bengal or China Roses.

Agrippina, deep crimson.
Archduke Charles, changeable.
Eugene Beauharnais, rich crimson.
Indica Alba, white daily.
Madam Preon, fine rose.
Lucullus, dark crimson.
Pink Daily.
Louis Philippe, crimson and rose.
Sanguinea, blood-red.

Noisette Roses.

Augusta, pale yellow.
Amie Vibert, pure white.
Beauty of Green Mount, deep rose color.
Gloire de Dijon, bronze yellow, with orange center.
Lamarque, large, pure white.
La Pactole, pale yellow.
Setina, bright pink.
Solfaterre, yellowish white.
Souvenir de Anselm, clear carmine, very fragrant.
Washington, clear white.

Tea Scented Roses.

Alba Rosea, white, with rose center.
Amabilis, rose color.
Belle Alamande, blush.
Bougere, salmon rose, bronzed.
Bon Silene, purple, shaded to carmine.
Marechal Niel, golden yellow, sweetest of the sweet.
Cornelia Cook, canary yellow.
Devoniensis, creamy white.
Leveson Gower, rosy salmon.
Madame Falcot, nankeen yellow.
Madame de Vatrey, carmine rose.
Pauline Lebonte, light blush.
Safrano, bright buff, very free bloomer.
Triomphe de Luxembourg, rose color.
White Tea, pure white, blooms freely.

Moss Roses.—Perpetual.

Perpetual White, very fine.
Madame Edward Ory, deep rose.
Maupertius, velvety-red, very dark.
Raphael, blush, large clusters.
Salet, bright rose.
Souvenir de Pierre Vibert, dark red, shaded with violet.

Annual Moss Roses.

English Moss, old variety, very mossy.
Adelaide, crimson.
Glory of Mosses, rose color; fine.
Alice Leroy, pale lilac.
Luxembourg, crimson.
Henry Martin, brilliant carmine.

Prairie Roses.—Hardy Climbers.

Baltimore Belle, nearly white.
Queen of the Prairie, rosy red.
Seven Sisters, crimson, shading to white.
Gem of the Prairies, a hybrid between the Queen of the Prairie and Madame Laffay; a strong, vigorous grower, flowers rich rosy crimson, and of delicious fragrance. A great acquisition to climbing roses.

The oldest Rose Bush in the world is said to be one which is trained upon one side of the Cathedral of Hildesheim, in Germany. Its age is unknown, but documents exist which prove that a Bishop Hezelio, nearly a thousand years ago, protected it by a stone roof, which is still in existence. The largest Rose Bush is a white Banksia, in the Marine Garden at London, which was sent there, the first of its kind, in 1813, by Bonpland. Its numerous branches, some of which measure eighteen inches in circumference, cover an immense wall to a width of nearly sixty feet, and at times, in early Spring, as many as fifty thousand flowers have been counted on this Queen of all Roses!

> " Roses are of royal birth,
> Loveliest monarchs of the earth!
> Not the realm of flowers alone,
> But human hearts their sceptre own.
> Mark what flowers the maiden's hand
> Gathers for her bridal band;
> What the sweetest influence shed,
> Round the grateful sufferer's bed;
> What with holiest light illume
> The grief and darkness of the tomb."

CHAPTER IX.

Ornamental Vines.

"Flowers! bright, beautiful, love-beaming flowers,
They are linked with life's sweetest and sunniest hours;
Like stars about our pathway
They shine so pure and fair,
Blooming in rich profusion,
Greeting us everywhere."

Trees and flowers are not enough with which to adorn and beautify our surroundings; we must have vines, an abundance of vines. A house without vines is like a bird without a mate; it wears a look of desolation. Vines grow so thriftily, bloom so profusely, and can be twined into so many beautiful forms — are so fresh, blooming and fragrant—that they should be trained about every house. The most modest little cot can be transformed into a flowery bower by the aid of a few climbing plants. Your homes may lack the paint, gilding and tapestry that adorn those of your neighbors, but if vines are trained over the doors and windows, they will present a fresh beauty and glory every Summer's morn, which the products of art cannot surpass.

Nature has given us the means of adorning our surroundings, and they are innocent, animating, and contribute to our piety towards her. We do not half avail ourselves of the cheap riches wherewith she adorns the earth. A few seeds, for instance, and a little trouble, would clothe our houses every Summer as high as we choose, with draperies of green and scarlet, and after admiring the beauty we might eat the produce. But then this produce is a bean, and beans are vulgar. Nobody despises a vine in front of a house, for vines are polite, and the grapes seldom good enough to be of use. Hops are like vines, yet who thinks of adorning his house with them? No, they also are vulgar! Thus writes Leigh Hunt in his flowery "Essays." There are many despised things that are, if properly cultivated, capable of great beauty; but I should prefer the Scarlet Bean as a covering to my pantry windows, and the Hop and Grape Vine to trail over the kitchen garden wall, while the Morning Glory, with all its wealth of entangled vines and flowers, should throw its radiance around the dining-room piazza, and shield its windows from the scorching sun at noonday. These same Morning Glories are glories indeed, and are not half appreciated. The delicate Japonica receives far more attention than its coarser parent, but it is infested with bugs, which make it a nuisance, while none dare as yet to molest my "Glories."

We pay high prices for exotic vines and climbing roses, and let the lovely vines of our own woods remain uncultivated in their wildness. There is no country that does not possess rarely beautiful vines, which well reward the cultivator with their luxuriant beauty. They are scattered from the White Mountains to the Gulf of Mexico, and all through the Western States on to the Pacific Slope.

Climbing roses are bowers of beauty for a few weeks, but after that are only briars, wormy and miserable. There is little beauty in their foliage; it is all compressed in their flowers; yet the Prairie Rose is more commonly used to twine over a verandah, while the Wistaria, Jasmine, Woodbine, Honeysuckle, etc., are planted in less conspicuous places, or not at all.

I delight in Climbing Roses—do not think I would disparage them—but they are far prettier the greater part of the year, if trained to pillars rather than to piazzas. Ampelopsis quinquefolia (Virginia Creeper or Five-Fingered Ivy), is a very hardy vine that will withstand the coldest New England winter. It grows most rapidly, and its dark green foliage, which changes to scarlet and brown in the Autumn, makes it very desirable for piazzas, rustic arbors, or trellis work. It will cling to brick walls as readily as the English Ivy; it is perfectly free from insects, and so flexible that it can be trained to any position.

Akebia quinata is an imported vine from Japan, with gracefully cut foliage, and large clusters of very fragrant, chocolate colored flowers. It is perfectly hardy.

Aristolochia Sipho (or Dutchman's Pipe), is a handsome climber for verandahs; its flowers resemble a short-stemmed pipe, are of a brownish hue, and the leaves are very large and of a bright green. It requires a rich soil to grow well.

Bignonia radicans (or Trumpet Creeper), is a very showy, robust plant, and produces a profusion of reddish-orange flowers. It is well adapted to plant against old trees, or to cover unsightly walls.

Bignonia grandiflora is fine for pillars or trellises, being of a more graceful habit than the radicans.

Bignonia Venusta is a very beautiful half-hardy climber, but requires age to perfect its blossoms, which are of a beautiful orange scarlet. For the Southern States it is unsurpassed in beauty, but for the Northern it needs the protection of a greenhouse.

Jasminum nudiflorum (or Carolina Jessamine), is tender north of Maryland, but is one of the most attractive vines in the United States. Its plentiful yellow flowers are rarely fragrant, and it grows in profusion all through the South, turning its luxuriant branches among the forests. No matter whether it is located in the piney barrens, or the rich swamp lands, it is a bower of beauty.

Celastrus scandens (or Bitter-sweet), is a very attractive climber, particularly in the Autumn, when its orange berries are very handsome. The scarlet seed-covers are surrounded with orange-colored capsules, which open as the seeds become ripe, and make it very ornamental. It twines so close to the trees that it will frequently choke out the life of young saplings. In Massachusetts it is called Roxbury Wax Work. It grows abundantly all through New England, and bears transplanting and cultivating with good effect.

Cocculus Carolinus is a native of the Carolinas, and has bright red fruit, resembling the common currant.

Of Honeysuckles (or Loniceras), we have a numerous variety. The scarlet or coral species are well-known, and the fragrant pink and white monthly is very popular. Of late years different varieties have been imported from China and Japan, which are very desirable. Among the Chinese, the Golden Leaved Lonicera is one of the finest. It is a rapid grower, with small wiry stems, the foliage is netted with gold, the flowers are white and very fragrant.

Lonicera Halliana is evergreen; its flowers pure white, turning to yellow; perfectly hardy, and flowers monthly in profuse clusters.

Lonicera brachypoda, or Japan Honeysuckle, is a very beautiful vine;

its flowers are of the most delicious fragrance, and there is no hardy vine that can excel it; its leaves are evergreen, and very glossy.

The Clematis are rapid growers, the native varieties flowering in August when other vines are not always in beauty. Great improvements have been made in them by the English florists, and there are no lovelier vines for piazzas and verandahs. The following are the most prominent of the cultivated varieties, flowering from June onward:

Clematis Fortuni has very large, double-white flowers.

Clematis Jackmanii is a profuse bloomer, with large, violet-colored blossoms.

Clematis Standishii is blue, and flowers finely.

Clematis Rubella has rich purple blossoms.

All of these varieties are new hybrids, and cannot fail to give satisfaction to the cultivator.

Hedera helix (or English Ivy), is the most popular of evergreen vines, and very suitable for covering rock work, fences, walls, trees or arbors. It adheres readily to a tree or to stone, but does not take as kindly to brick, requiring some slight support, frequently to keep it attached to the walls. It is much used for covering houses, but in climates where it will live throughout the year it is unequaled for a bordering to flower beds. Grass will force its tiny roots into the borders, but the Ivy is contented to twine its branches along the edges. A quantity of strong young plants are desirable to commence with, and they should be planted rather thickly and kept well mingled together. In the Summer, their fresh green leaves contrast perfectly with the darker foliage, and all through the winter their verdure is pleasing. Such edgings form a beautiful setting for flowers, while they are so charming as to make it desirable to cultivate the "dainty plant" for its own worth.

After the edging has once become established, by pinching off and cutting back the young shoots, it can be easily kept in perfect order. Nearly every courtyard in Paris displays the English Ivy, either covering trellises as a dark background to brilliant thickets of Geraniums, or trained over a bower.

The plants are grown in large boxes, filled with a rich turfy soil, and thus supplied they make rapid growth. At the French Exposition, the garden was filled with all that was richest and rarest, yet Mr. Robinson tells us, in his book upon "French Gardens," that a pretty circular bower covered with Ivy attracted first the attention of every passer-by.

It was composed of a wire frame, shaped like an umbrella, with the handle inserted in a huge tub of very rich earth, in which the roots were planted. Boards were laid over the tub, which formed a circular seat, and with these simple means a most lovely bower was produced. The Ivy was trained so as to-cover every part of it, and entirely shade the seat. Any ingenious boy could make a similar one, and, with proper appliances, some girls could accomplish it.

As a screen, this plant is in great demand in France, and entire garden walls are often covered with it, making a most perfect background for the brilliant hues of the flowers.

Those of us who live in colder climates could substitute the German Ivy for edgings. I tried it last season, and it grew beautifully, but it will winter kill. An old umbrella frame, stripped of its dilapidated covering, will make a fine trellis for delicate vines like the Canary Bird Flower, Thunbergia, Maurandya, and Cypress Vine.

Sharpen the handle to a point, and fix it firmly in the ground, pressing in the ivory tip of each end, so that the wind cannot disturb it. It will look prettily on the lawn, or in the center bed of the garden, when the graceful twining vines have covered it with their beautiful flowers and foliage, and almost every garret can furnish the skeleton, if the closet cannot provide one.

A worn-out sunshade will make a baby trellis that will be very charming, when covered with the gorgeous hues of the Tropæolum, which should not be neglected in a chapter upon Vines. They grow readily from seed, and their butterfly-colored flowers are always beautiful. If branches are broken off in the Autumn, and put into vases filled with water, the flowers will bloom for a long time; the roots starting out at each joint will furnish a support for them.

Cobæa scandens is a rapid growing vine, with large purple bell-shaped flowers. It is not hardy in the Northern States, but can be kept in pots during the Winter, and will twine over the windows.

Cobæa scandens variegata is like the former, only its leaves are margined with yellowish-white. If planted in rich soil, these vines can be made to grow thirty feet in a season.

Glycine Sinensis (or Chinese Wistaria), is a very elegant vine of quick growth; it has long, pendulous clusters of pale blue flowers both in the Spring and Autumn, and will soon cover a large surface.

Wistaria Sinensis Alba is a white variety, not so robust as the blue.

Wistaria Frutescens (or American Glycine), is more of a dwarf habit than the above-mentioned.

Passiflora Incarnata (Half Hardy Passion Vine), is very beautiful. Its flower is supposed to represent the Crucifixion of Christ, and thence its name.

Periploca Græca (Virginia Silk Vine), is another native climber that deserves attention, in preference to many that are tender. It is a hardy grower, and will soon cover an arbor or wall. A native of Syria.

Care and attention must be given to the training and fastening of all climbers, as their beauty is greatly injured by allowing them to grow in a wild and neglected manner; it also gives a wild look to a house, which does not add to its general appearance.

Wherever there is an unsightly fence, there is the opportunity to try your hand at cultivating vines which grow wild in your woods, or which can be raised from seeds at a trifling expense. Wreath all such places with climbing vines, and let their ugliness be hid under the delicate foliage and brilliant flowers of the climbers. Your wood, brick, or stone houses are bare in their angular outlines, and lack the graceful elegance which ornamental vines will give them. Twine over them some climbing plant, and architecture and nature will combine to produce the most picturesque effect; and you will learn that—

"The flowers in silence seem to breathe
Such thoughts as language cannot tell."

And when the outside is beautiful, let the inside be replete with comfort, order, taste, virtue, peace, good-will and love.

The following diagrams will furnish designs for supports for Ornamental Vines. They can be made from six to eight feet high. The center piece of each trellis should be thicker than the outer or main supports, at least three-quarters of an inch thick, and from an inch to an inch-and-a-half wide. These frames should be painted green or white, according to one's preference.

68 *EVERY WOMAN HER OWN FLOWER GARDENER.*

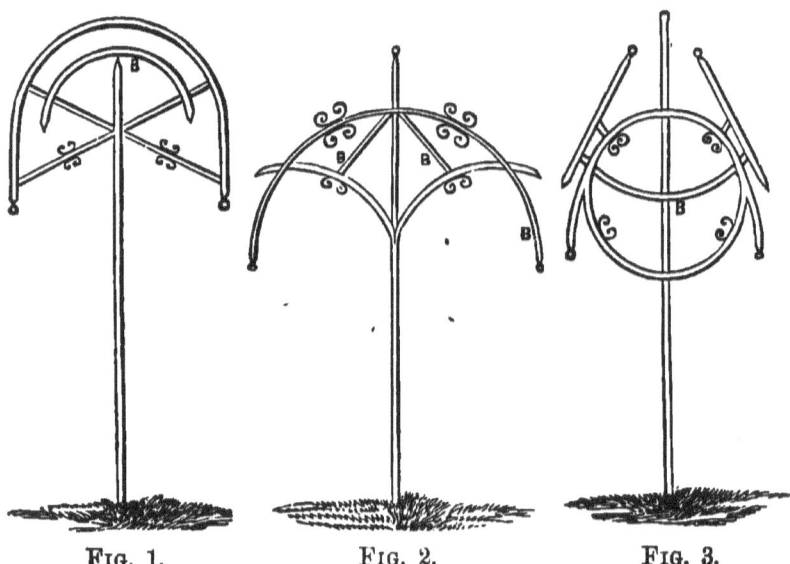

FIG. 1. FIG. 2. FIG. 3.

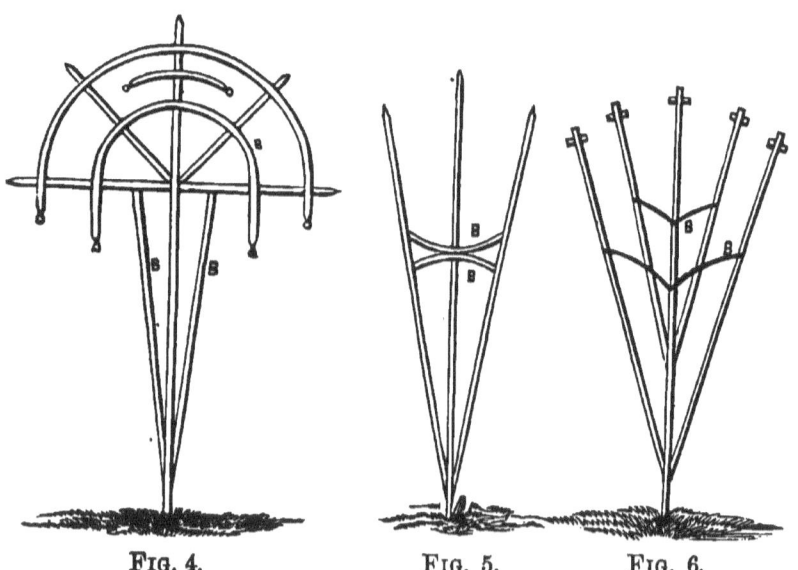

FIG. 4. FIG. 5. FIG. 6.

CHAPTER X.

ORNAMENTAL SHRUBS FOR GARDEN AND LAWN.

"Thank God for the beautiful Flowers
That blossom so sweetly and fair;
They garnish this strange life of ours,
And brighten our paths every where;
They speak of the heaven above us,
Where angels are singing His praise,
Where dwell the dear ones who love us,
Who faded from earth's thorny ways."

Shrubs are indispensable in the smallest collection of plants. Many of them are early risers, and bloom as soon as the frost and ice have disappeared. Once obtained and planted out in good, rich soil, they require but little attention, and will bloom for years in the same locality. Yet their foliage and flowers will be more luxuriant and beautiful, if they are treated to a few shovelsful of compost or manure, yearly. If it is given to them in the autumn, it acts as a protection from the frost, and can be dug into their roots early in the spring. When they are first planted, it is better to take the autumn rather than the spring for the operation; but if done in March or April (according to the climate), be sure to mulch the roots with long stable litter, or a few inches deep of hay; this will keep them from drying up during the heat of summer.

The Flowering Almond takes first rank, because it blooms so early, and though very common, is always popular. If it is neglected it will grow ill-shaped and scraggy, but if it is cut back as soon as its blossoms are fallen, its increased growth will soon repay their sacrifice.

The Flowering Plum is called by some the White Flowering Almond, and is equally hardy, its flowers being as double as those of the Almond, and of a snowy whiteness.

The Lilac is always admired, will always be cultivated; every house must have at least one or more of these shrubs. The purple variety is seen everywhere; the white is not quite as common, and is not as sickishly sweet as the purple.

The Persian and Chinese Lilacs are more beautiful than the common kinds. The former is a small tree of graceful habit, and its flowers are of a lighter lilac color. The latter is especially desirable, the flowers are much darker than the other varieties, and its foliage is of a dark glossy green, very rich. These shrubs are perfectly hardy, and are usually grown without any care, yet if pruned and manured their beauty will be much increased.

Cydonia Japonica, or Scarlet-flowered Japan Quince, is also a well-known shrub, producing quantities of the richest scarlet flowers close to its branches; it is indispensable in every garden.

Calycanthus floridus, or Allspice Flower, is an old favorite, not so often cultivated in these latter days. Its foliage is of a light glossy green, and its flowers are of the darkest maroon, and very fragrant; both blossoms and branches possess a strong spicy flavor, and it is sometimes called the Strawberry Shrub, from a fancied resemblance to the odor of that berry.

Forsythia viridissima is one of the earliest of all shrubs in blossoming; its bright golden-lined flowers appear before the leaves are hardly visible, and completely cover the branches.

Flowering Acacia, with its profusion of pink and white pea-shaped blossoms, is always welcome. Its foliage is deeply serrated like the Locust leaves; its habit is straggling, which detracts from its beauty.

Hydrangea quercifolia, or Oak-leaved Hydrangea, has strongly marked foliage, and its blossoms are in large panicles of white flowers. It blooms in July, and is a great attraction on a lawn.

Hydrangea deutziafolia is a recent importation from Japan. Its leaves resemble those of the Deutzia; it blooms in August, bearing very large panicles of snowy white flowers, which change to pink, and finally to a brownish purple. It is a valuable addition to a garden or lawn.

The Deutzias are generally cultivated, and are always beautiful.

Deutzia gracilis is perfectly hardy, and has plentiful clusters of pure white flowers. Deutzia scrabra is of larger growth, often attains to five or six feet, and is covered with clusters of blossoms, which resemble the Orange flower without its fragrance.

Deutzia crenata flore pleno produces double flowers, white in the center, and red in the outer leaves. It is of a strong habit, desires plenty of room to grow in, and will often be seen over six feet high, and when in flower is "a thing of beauty." All these species of Deutzias are hardy, but at the far north require a little protection in winter.

Mahonia Aquifolium is an elegant, evergreen shrub. Its foliage is evergreen, and of a dark rich purplish green. Its flowers are bright yellow, and appear early in the spring.

The Privet or Prim is also desirable, its foliage is attractive, and its small clusters of white flowers add much to its beauty.

Philadelphus inodorus, or Mock Orange, is a more delicate species of the Syringa. It bears large, pure white flowers with rich yellow stamens, along its slender stems, covering the shrub with a wealth of bloom. It will grow eight feet high, and blossoms in June.

The Wiegelas are well established favorites, and deservedly so; for their brightly colored flowers, intermixed with the glossy green foliage, produce a fine effect either in the flower bed or on the lawn.

Wiegela nivea produces pure white flowers, very beautiful for large bouquets and vases.

Wiegela rosea bears apple-blossom colored flowers, blending pink and white in a lovely intermingling.

Wiegela alba has white flowers, which change to a pale rose tint.

Spiræas are of a most numerous family. The florists have cultivated them with great success, and wherever the Lilac and the Syringa flourish they will grow and bloom in perfection.

Their flowers are of various shades of color, from pure white, white tinged with pink, yellowish white, purple rose, lilac, pink, etc.

Spiræa salicifolia grows from two to five feet high; is white, tinted with rose, and blooms in June and July.

Spiræa opulifolia, five to seven feet high; white flowers, with rosy tint.

Spiræa Reevesii, one of the most beautiful of its family, flowers in June in pure white clusters.

Spiræa Bella, dwarf; pink flowers.

Spiræa Japonica is also dwarf, and bears feather plumes of white flowers in June.

Tartarian Honeysuckles are large shrubs of much beauty, whether covered with their pink or white flowers, or with scarlet berries. They will grow from cuttings or seeds, and require little care. The two varieties planted together make a fine wall for a garden, and serve as a protection from the north winds. There are several shrubs which bear brightly-colored berries, which make them conspicuous objects in garden or lawn; so in making up a collection of shrubs we should not forget them.

Euonymus, or Strawberry Tree, is very handsome, with its purple flowers, succeeded by brilliant scarlet berries curiously shaped, which remain on the branches late into the Autumn. The Burning Bush is the common name for it in many localities. A variety of this shrub or tree grows in most of the Middle, Western and Southern States.

Euonymus atropurpureus, or Spindle Tree, is its proper title. It is a very beautiful addition to every lawn. The European Burning Bush is much inferior to our native variety. The Broad-Leaved Burning Bush is a native of Austria; its botanical name is Euonymus latifolius, and it is not commonly grown in this country, but is very desirable.

The Black Alder bears berries of a flame-like scarlet, close to its branches, and is a beautiful shrub.

I have endeavored to mention a few of the flowering shrubs that will not fail to give satisfaction to all amateur gardeners. Many of them are old-time flowers, which possess a charm to me, as childish associations of delight linger about them, and render them doubly dear.

The Rhododendrons are extensively cultivated, and greatly improved from those which grow wild in the Middle States. The English florists have brought these beautiful shrubs to the highest state of perfection.

The Rose of Sharon is one of the most beautiful foreign shrubs. Its blossoms are bell-shaped, and of many mingled hues. In Syria, Judea and Arabia it is a sacred flower, and they have adopted it as the emblem of the Resurrection. The dried flower is placed by the inhabitants of Judea in a vase of water beside the beds of the sick; if it expands, the omen is favorable, but if not, death is considered inevitable.

The Yucca Filamentosa, rather a hardy herbaceous plant, though a shrub, is very ornamental and hardy, its foliage resembling that of the Aloe. It blooms in August and September, and the flower stem rises to the height of five or six feet, surmounted with white, bell-shaped flowers. It grows well in common garden soil, and is very desirable as a single plant on the lawn.

All of these shrubs are most agreeable additions to every flower garden, but if you cannot find room for all, be sure to select a few of them, for no other plants will give you as large a supply of flowers with so little attention expended on them. Most of them will readily grow from cuttings, all of them will layer easily, and many of them increase by suckers from the roots.

CHAPTER XI.

THE CARNATION, AND PICOTEE PINKS.

"Ye are the Scriptures of the earth,
Sweet flowers, fair and frail;
A sermon speaks in every bud,
That woos the summer gale."

The Carnation has been cultivated from time immemorial in Europe, and from Gerard, the herbalist of Queen Elizabeth's time, we learn some of its quaint old English names, such as "Sops in Wine" (very expressive of the variegated red and white flower), "Pagaiants," "Horseflesh," "Blunkets," etc.

The most common varieties of the Carnation sprung from the Clove Gilliflower, or Clove Pink, and in former days was much used to distil Clove Gilliflower Water, which was in great repute as a restorative. The florists divide them into three classes now—flakes, bizarres and picotees.

The flakes, on a pure yellow or white ground, have only one color, disposed in broad flashes or stripes, and extending the length of the petal.

The bizarres, on a pure white or yellow ground, have two or more colors in irregular stripes of pink, or scarlet and purple, sometimes running from the base to the margin of the petal, sometimes broken irregularly into spots.

The Picotee was formerly spotted with purple, red or scarlet spots, on a white or yellow ground; modern improvements have changed its character; it is no longer a spotted carnation, but one with the colorings confined to a bordering of each petal.

Each of these three classes are sub-denominated according to their colors, as scarlet-flake, pink-flake, scarlet-bizarre, etc., etc.

The stripes or spots in Carnations are usually in shades of scarlet, pink and purple, on a white, pink, red or yellow ground.

The word "Carnation" is fully significant of the flesh-color which characterized the original and earlier cultivated varieties.

Of all the flowers that adorn the garden, whether they charm the eye by their beauty, or regale the sense of smelling by their fragrance, the Carnation may justly rank next to the Rose.

The Flemish weavers, who sought a refuge in England from the religious persecutions of Philip II, and the cruelty of the Duke of Alva, were renowned for their Carnations, Roses, and Gilliflowers, and they introduced many of the rarest varieties of these flowers, often superior to the specimens produced by professional gardeners. Mr. Hogg, a celebrated florist, and also a writer upon Floriculture, declares that "it is not every gardener who knows how to grow a Carnation, and there is not one in ten whose assistance I would claim on the most pressing occasion, and leave the operation of layering to them unlooked after; whereas I would implicitly trust it to any weaver, cobbler or barber who had had the least practice with his own flowers."

There is hardly any plant grown by florists to which they consider a congenial soil is of so much importance. It should be composed of one-half rotten horse manure, not less than a year old; that which has been used in a hot-bed is just the article for composing the soil for Carnations. Add to it one-third fresh loam, and one-third coarse river sand. If these ingredients are mixed together in the Autumn, and allowed to freeze, and in the Spring are thoroughly mixed up, a good compost will be obtained. Those of our readers who live near a florist had better buy the compost for their plants. Large piles of it are always kept on hand, and sold cheaply. It is better to supply the soil for all pot plants in this way. Carnations are propagated by seed, layers and cuttings.

The seed should be sown in April or May, in pots filled with rich compost, and a little fine sand, barely sufficient to cover them, sprinkled over the seeds. As soon as the young plants are three inches high, they should be planted out into a bed of rich soil. They will not bloom until the following Summer, but the plants can be protected in cold climates by laying sods of grass over them, or by keeping the plants in the cellar in boxes.

The best time to layer is when the plant is in full bloom, which will be about the middle of July, or according to the season. The shoot to be layered may be four or five joints in length; all the lower leaves next to the root must be stripped off, leaving only those on the two or three upper joints. The surface of the soil should be stirred up to the depth of an inch; then take the shoot in the finger and thumb of the left hand, and bend it upwards, so that the knife can enter a quarter of an inch below the second or third joint from the top, and on the side of the shoot next the ground; cut upwards through the center of the joint, slantingly for about half an inch. Now cut off the tip of the portion underneath close to the joint. If it breaks off it is worthless as a layer, so handle it very carefully, and lay the shoot into the soil, pegging it down with a large hair pin. The root fibres are soonest formed when the joint is but lightly covered with earth, not more than a quarter of an inch. No more of the stem of the layer than just close to the joint, nor any of the leaves should be buried in the soil, for the dampness will cause them to decay, and the whole layer will then damp off or decay.

When the layer is pegged down, give it a gentle watering, taking care not to wash off the soil.

It is of no consequence if the layer does not stand straight at first. It will soon grow so.

If the plants are kept moist, and well shaded from the noonday heat, the layers will be rooted in three or four weeks. They should then be cut away from the plant, with about half an inch of the stem which connects them to it, and planted in five-inch pots.

Great care must be taken not to injure the tiny roots, nor break the part of the stem above the incision.

In raising Carnations from cuttings, good healthy shoots should be selected, and they should be treated as described for other cuttings.

Layering and raising from cuttings are the surest modes of propagating fine varieties. It is said that the chance of obtaining a good Carnation from seed is one to a hundred.

The culture of the Picotee, or Paisley Pink, is the same as that of the Carnation. The Picotee is the hardier of the two, and will endure the cold winters without covering, excepting at the extreme north.

When the flower stems are ten or more inches high, they should be supported with stakes, and when the flowers appear, if there is danger of their bursting the calyx, and thus spoiling their symmetry, it is well to tie a bit of colored worsted yarn about them; this gives support, and retains the leaves in place. Monthly Carnations are the most desirable of all kinds, as they bloom during the winter.

A select list of monthly varieties:—

Admirable, creamy white.
Astoria, yellow, flaked with scarlet.
Attraction, white, striped with maroon.
Betsey, brilliant scarlet.
Blondin, buff and rose.
D'Fontana, buff, striped with cherry.
Donadi's Pride, white, edged with pink; fine.
Edwardsii, pure white; extra.
Grant, rich crimson, striped with slate color.
Grand Conde, white, blotched with rose.
La Purite, bright rosy pink.
Ma Gloire, sulphur yellow, striped scarlet.
Queen of Whites, purest white.
Radetzky, rose color with broad purple stripes.
Star, carmine, splashed with white.
Gen. Von Moltke, orange salmon, flaked with scarlet.
Rosaline, bright buff, blotched with crimson.
Vaillante, scarlet fringed, dwarf, profuse bloomer.
Welcome, brightest red, perfect shape.

CHAPTER XII

HERBACEOUS PLANTS, PÆONIES, PHLOXES, CHRYSANTHEMUMS,
DELPHINIUMS, AND A SELECT LIST OF DESIRABLES.

> "There is a lesson in each flower,
> A story in each stream and bower;
> On every herb on which you tread
> Are written words which, rightly read,
> Will lead you from earth's fragrant sod,
> To hope, and holiness, and God."

Herbaceous Plants are Perennials, which die down to the roots every winter, but in the spring, send up fresh stems and blossoms from the roots, thereby furnishing the easiest means of adorning a garden. They require but very little care, as the most of them are hardy, while others require a slight protection. The soil should be kept in good order, free from weeds, and a yearly dressing of good compost will make them bloom luxuriantly, and some species are so vigorous that they will continue to bloom annually, even in a neglected grass sod. Many of them bloom early in the season, as soon as the Snowdrop. Crocus and Hyacinth have passed away; and by a judicious selection, a profuse and gorgeous supply of flowers may be obtained from a bed of these plants, until the garden is brilliant with the brightly tinted Annuals, etc.

A list of the most desirable of these plants will be given, with their time of flowering; but I must first call your attention to the Herbaceous Pæonies, which form a large family of most beautiful flowers, some of which are indispensable in the smallest collection of plants.

Herbaceous Pæonies.

The common red Pæony, or, as it is usually called in the old-fashioned parlance among those of an older generation, Piny, used to grow in every country garden; its large and brilliant red flowers rendering it very conspicuous, and delighting all lovers of gorgeous colorings. Well do I remember the *furore* caused among amateur florists by the introduction of a white Pæony, and every one must have a root of it, to contrast with their fiery-red flowers.

Then the fragrant pink variety was introduced and much admired; and for many years no other novelty appeared in their ranks; but the English and French florists were busily engaged in cultivating these flowers, and now over one hundred varieties are given in the catalogues, and described as distinct in shape, hue, time of flowering, etc.

The Pæony is very showy when planted by itself, yet when grown *en masse*, the effect is truly magnificent. The darkest shades should be arranged in the center of the bed, and the colors shaded out to pure white; thus planted, a beautiful show can be obtained.

Alba Plenaia, very double flower, white.
Whitleyi, older variety, very fragrant, white with yellow center.
Virginalis, of the purest white.
Baron Rothschild, flower large, pale rose.
Queen Victoria, rose color.
Amabilis, outer petals rose color, and the inner a delicate, creamy white.
Festiva, white, shaded to carmine red in the center.
Albicans Plena, rosy pink, and blooms early and late
Maiden's Blush, fine and large, bright pink.
Duchesse d'Orleans, outside petals violet-rose, and deep salmon buff at the center.
Pomponia, of a purplish pink, with salmon colored center
Pattsii, very rich, darkest purplish crimson.
Duchesse de Nemours, rosy lilac.
Tenuifolia, funnel-shaped leaves, flowers deep crimson
Pompadoura, dark crimson, inner petals delicately cut.
Rubra Striata, richest rosy crimson.

The Moutan or Tree Pæonies are very beautiful; they are perfectly hardy, excepting in northern New England, where, to bloom in perfection, they should be covered with a barrel filled with leaves. They do not die down to the roots every winter, and are more properly called shrubs.

Phloxes.

The beauty of these Herbaceous Plants is not fully appreciated. They are perfectly hardy, and their brilliant clusters of flowers, comprising all colors from white to crimson and purple, striped and mottled, have few superiors among hardy plants. They will thrive in almost any soil, but enjoy fresh loam, and new quarters every two or three years. They increase rapidly from the roots, will also grow easily from cuttings or layers.

Select list of varieties:—
Albert Cameron, large white flower, with carmine eye.
Alexandrine Bellet de Varenne, carmine, with scarlet center.
Augustine Lierval, white, pink center.
Chloris, vivid red.
Countess of Home, white, dark crimson center.
L'Orientale, amoranth, large flower, extra.
Madame Thaman, rich carmine, crimson center.
Madame d'Argent, rose colored, purple center.
Madame Henricq, velvety rose, carmine eye.
Mademoiselle Lemichez, white, scarlet center.
Monsieur Audry, very bright red.
Roi Leopold, striped rose and white, very showy.
Raphael, rose, crimson eye.
White Lady, new, pure white, with clusters of flowers six inches in diameter.
Surpasse Marie Belanger, large, white, purple eye.

Chrysanthemums.

These come into bloom so late in the season that they are frequently called the "Christmas flower"; and, as they fill a place occupied by no other flower, should therefore be cultivated in every garden.

They are most easily propagated from cuttings, taken in August, or from the shoots sent up from the roots after blooming. They are very hardy excepting at the extreme north, and can be wintered there under sods. Good specimens should have but one stem, with short, thick-set branches, which may be made to grow by pinching off the end shoots, thus encouraging the side branches. They grow very vigorously in a rich light soil.

There are three varieties or species; the large flowered, most suitable for out-door culture; the dwarf or Pompone, which blooms beautifully, in-doors, and their different colors will form a choice bouquet; and the Japan Chrysanthemums. All of these species are beautiful objects in the open garden in November and December.

Large flowering varieties:—
Boule d'Or, fine, large, golden yellow.
Boule d'Neige, large, pure white.
Captivation, light purple, splendid.
Erecta Superba, clear sulphur-yellow.
Lord Derby, deep purple, petals incurved.
Guernsey Nugget, light yellow.
Princess Teck, creamy white.
Prince Albert, crimson, red.
Queen of England, blush.
Mount Ætna, fiery crimson.
Princess of Wales, purest white.
Temple of Solomon, golden yellow.

Pompone or Liliputian Chrysanthemums.

Acton, golden yellow.
Countesse de Mons, pale rose.
Iris, white tipped with rose.
Sinbad, light crimson.
Mad. De Soulangis, pure rose.
Trevenna, purest white.
Roi de Liliput, maroon.
Theresita, fine, lilac.
Ragozza, yellow, tipped with rose.

Japan Chrysanthemums.

These flowers are novelties, from Japan—with tasselled or quilled flowers.

Laciniatus, is creamy white, fine for bouquets and vases.
Mons. Bonnet, amber, fine large flowers.

These plants are of an elegant appearance, and by pinching off the first flower buds, can be made to bloom in January and February.

Delphiniums, or Hardy Perennial Larkspurs,
Are among the finest of this class of plants, and if the seed-pods are cut off, will continue in flower from July to November. They will also flower the first year if sown early in hot-bed, and are very desirable for late blooming. They grow readily from seed or from the increase of the root. The shades of blue are unsurpassed by any other flower of similar color.

Delphinium Formosum is of the brightest blue with a white center.
D. Mons. Neuner, pale blue.
D. Chinensi Pumilum, azure blue.
D. Alba, paper white.
D. Belladonna, finest sky blue.

A list of Herbaceous Plants that will give a succession of flowers.

Achillea Millefolium Rubrum, deep red, one foot high, blooms from June to September.

Achillea Ptarmica Plena, pure white double flowers, in bloom from July to October.

Aconitum Napellus (Monkshood), dark blue; four to six feet; June to August.

Aconitum Versicolor, variegated, blue and white; three to five feet; July to August.

Arabis Alpina, pure white flowers, eight inches; May.

Asclepias tuberosa, orange colored flowers; two feet; July.

Amsonia salicifolia, lavender blue, in clusters; three feet; June.

Anemone Japonica, purplish rose; eighteen inches; September.

Aquilegia jocunda (Columbine), dark blue, white center; two feet; June.

Aquilegia striata, striped, blue and white.

Aquilegia Sibirica, dark bluish-black flowers, very double; one foot; June.

Baptisia cerulea, brightest blue; two feet; June.

Baptisia alba, flowers pure white; two feet; June.

Bocconia cordata, very showy, large foliage, spikes of whitish flowers; six to eight feet; July.

Callirrhoe involucrata, trailing plant with bright crimson flowers; June.

Hollyhocks, very double flowers, all colors; July to October.

Lupinus polyphyllus, flowers of various colors, from pure white to the darkest purple; two to three feet; July.

Lychnis albo pleno, double, white; a foot and a half high; May and June.

Lychnis Chalcedonica pleno, double, scarlet; two to three feet; June and July.

Lychnis Haagena, all colors from white to scarlet.

Orobus vernus, reddish purple; one foot; April and May.

Papaver Orientale, brilliant scarlet flowers; three feet; June and July.

Penstemon grandiflora; there are many varieties from the Prairies; three feet; June.

Phalangium Liliago, flowers pure white, in loose spikes, elegant; two to three feet; July.

Saxifraga crassifolia, deep pink, in large clusters; six inches; blooms early in April.

Scutellaria Japonica, deep purplish blue; eight inches; July.

Lamium Maculatum album et Rubrum, flowers in short round spikes, red and white; June.

Zauschneria Californica, flowers of a bright scarlet, blossoms in July; hardy in middle States.

The varieties of the Funkia, or Day Lily, should not be omitted. The common variety is of a rare fragrance, and its flowers are produced in large clusters; only two or three of the pure white lilies opening at once. It is perfectly hardy in all climates. The variegated species has blueish-white flowers without the delicious odor of the white variety. Its leaves are prettily variegated, and are its chief attraction.

CHAPTER XIII.

IMMORTELLES, OR EVERLASTING FLOWERS, AND ORNAMENTAL GRASSES.

"There is religion in a flower:
Its still small voice is as the voice of conscience.
Mountains and oceans, planets, suns and systems,
Bear not the impress of Almighty power
In characters more legible than those
Which He hath written on the tiniest flower
Whose light bell bends beneath the dew-drop's weight."

No collection of flowers is complete without some few varieties of Immortelles, or Everlasting Flowers. When ice and snow abound, they serve to brighten our in-door surroundings. Mingled with dried grasses and branches of Arbor Vitæ, or some other evergreen, they make good substitutes for their more delicate sisters who are faded and gone.

My sitting room is always adorned, in the wintry season, with vases of these bright flowers, which retain their places until forced to yield them to the fragile flowers of the early spring.

So in ordering your seeds, don't forget to write down an assortment of these flowers, whose beauty is not evanescent.

They are invaluable decorations for home and church, and can be made into crowns, crosses and bouquets.

Their flowers should be gathered while in the bud; if allowed to expand, they will not be as handsome when dried. The stems should be tied together, and the bunches hung up in a dark, dry closet, taking care not to tie them up in too large quantities, to dry quickly, else they may mildew or mould. When well dried, put away in boxes until desired for use.

To save seeds from them, it is best to let the first blossoms remain uncut, and mature. When ripe, cut them off, and preserve until another season.

These plants will grow in any common garden soil. They are not particularly ornamental, as their flowers are kept well cut off, and it is better to plant a bed of them among the vegetables, or in some out-of-the-way corner, as they will not add to the beauty of your flower beds or lawns.

In the large cities, quite a trade is carried on in the way of these flowers, and thousands of them are yearly imported to supply the demand for crowns and crosses for the decoration of the cemeteries. At all seasons of the year they are appropriate there, for neither rain nor sun injures them, when well dried; while they, in their unfading brightness, fully corroborate their claims to the title of Immortelles.

The florists' catalogues offer us a good variety to select from, and at the head of the list stand the Acrocliniums—perhaps not quite as beautiful as Rhodanthe Manglesii, but easier of cultivation, as they are quite hardy, and not as delicate in habit.

They grow a foot high, and are of two kinds—a bright rose color, and pure white—each with a yellow center. The flowers are fragile enough to pass for "artificials," and they have been used in decorating ladies' hats, with good effect. Vases filled with them, and mingled with animated oats and grasses, are very ornamental. No garden should be without them.

Ammobium alatum is a white flower, which is very pretty in arranging memorial wreaths or crosses.

Globe Amaranth, or Gomphrena is commonly cultivated. It is found in shades from a bright orange to a purplish crimson, and pure white. The flowers should be gathered as soon as the colors are well developed.

Helichrysums are very desirable. They are in all varieties of color, from the brightest yellow, the purest white, to the richest shades of red. The minimum, or dwarf species, are the prettiest for wreaths, etc. Be sure to cut the buds, and they will dry into perfect flowers.

Helipterum Sanfordi is a later importation. Its flowers are of a bright golden yellow, and grow in small clusters of fine flowers, making an agreeable variety. Another kind produces snowy white flowers.

Rhodanthe is a charming everlasting. Its bright, bell shaped flowers and graceful habit make it an addition to the flower beds, as well as for winter decorations. There are four varieties.

Rhodanthe alba is of silvery whiteness, and the finest white Immortelle grown.

Rhodanthe atrosanguinea has dark crimson flowers, with a violet disc or center.

Rhodanthe Maculata has larger blossoms of a bright rose color, tinged with violet purple, with a yellow center. It is a fine plant for window gardening.

Rhodanthe Manglesii is the oldest variety. Its blossoms are rose colored, suffused with white. All these flowers are the most desirable of their kind. The silvery scales on the outside of the flower contrast charmingly with the brighter colors of the petals.

Waitzia aurea and grandiflora have flowers of a brilliant gold color, and produce a fine effect, when mingled with others. They bloom in clusters, and if left too long on the plant, become dingy and discolored.

Xeranthemums are very easily cultivated. The seeds vegetate as quickly as those of the Aster or Balsam. They are of various colors, and grow about one foot high, blooming very freely.

All of these plants require some space to grow in, and the plants must be transplanted at least a foot apart to bloom advantageously.

These Everlasting Flowers can be dyed into various colors. Last autumn some bright yellow Helichrysums fell into a solution of borax, and turned their petals to the most glorious sunset hue, with a fine metallic lustre. It oxydized the color, and my vases are still resplendent with the flowers. I tried its effect upon crimson and pink flowers, but it failed to beautify them, but faded out all their original brightness. The yellow flowers are of a wonderful golden-scarlet hue, rarely seen in any flower that grows. Dip the flowers into a cup of water into which as much borax as will dissolve has been added, and see for yourself the perfect shade of color. Family dyes can be used to dye purple, scarlet and green, and mosses can be thus prepared to arrange among the bright-hued flowers, making prettier objects for home adornment than can be purchased at the shops. Purple dye can be made at home from one ounce of ground logwood, one tablespoonful of powdered alum, and one pint of soft water; boil for twenty minutes; when cool, put in the flowers.

Yellow dye can be made with one ounce of quercitron bark; same proportions of alum and water as above; boil twenty minutes. Mix indigo with the yellow dye, and a beautiful green is formed, which will dye mosses or grasses perfectly.

Ornamental Grasses.

The varieties of grasses are almost innumerable. There are already known and described three thousand species in the world, and in America alone there are six hundred. On a small bit of turf, not a foot square, you may often find five or six different kinds. Our prairies abound in numerous varieties—some radiated, and variegated purple and green, like the peacock's plumage—others pinnated and feathery, as the marabout's plume; but all exceedingly beautiful!

The Durva grass of the Hindoos is one of the most perfect that is known.

Sir William Jones remarks that:—

"The flowers in their perfect state afford the loveliest object in creation; and when examined with a microscope, they resemble emeralds and rubies trembling in the slightest breath of air. Nor is the Durva less esteemed for its valuable qualities. It affords the sweetest and most nutritious pasturage for cattle; and its usefulness and beauty induced the Hindoos, even in the earliest ages, to believe that it was the dwelling place of a presiding and benevolent nymph, who loved to listen to the cropping of dewy herbage by flocks and herds in meadows, and beside clear streams. Poets feigned that looking forth from her diverging spike, adorned with purple flowers and ranged in two close, alternate rows, wherever she presided blights and mildews were unknown, and that the air was loaded with fragrance, as if from bowers of balm, although neither roses, citrons, richly scented magnolias, nor orange trees grew contiguous."

The Veda celebrates this inimitable grass in the following sentence of the A. E. harvana:—

"May the Durva, which arose from the waters of life, and which hath a hundred roots and a hundred stems, prolong my existence on earth for a hundred years."

Linnæus kneeled beside the northern holy grass, and thanked the Lord for having made it. Paley, the great moralist, loved the grasses, and delighted in the inspection of their tiny florets. And Christ taught us a lesson of faith from them, saying:—

"Wherefore, if God so clothe the grass of the field, which to-day is, and to-morrow is cast into the oven; shall He not much more clothe you, O ye of little faith?"

By grasses are meant all those plants which have a round, jointed, and hollow stem, surrounded at each joint with a single leaf, long, narrow and pointed, and whose seeds are contained in chaffy husks. This numerous family embraces even the tall Bamboo of India and the tropical climates, which affords building material for houses, furniture and carriages, and yet is brother to the meadow fox-tail grass.

The Ornamental Grasses are attracting more attention every year, and they are especially adapted to planting *en masse*, or in single beds on the lawn.

They are easily grown from seeds, which cost but a trifle. The perennial kinds are more desirable on account of their permanency; but there are many annual and biennial species well worthy of cultivation, even in the smallest garden. They add much to the attractiveness of bouquet or vase, and are truly numbered among the *indispensables*.

Andropogon Argenteum has silvery colored leaves and plumes of flowers; is quite hardy, grows four feet high, and is raised either from seeds or the division of its roots.

Andropogon bombycinus is a lovely novelty; with plumes covered with silky hairs of a metallic whiteness. It is a hardy perennial from Persia, growing one foot high.

Arundo donax versicolor has striped foliage, and is one of the most beautiful of grasses. It is not quite hardy, but should be covered with sods, or placed in a dry cellar during winter.

Chloropsis Blanchardia is a very elegant species, with rose colored spikes. It is also tender, requires protection in a northern climate.

Bromus brizæformis is a hardy species, with drooping panicles; grows one foot high.

Chascolytrum erectum is also hardy, and very ornamental; is a native of Chili; grows eighteen inches.

Chloris myriostachies is a new variety, with velvety flower heads; hardy; grows three feet.

Cyperus Paramatta belongs to the sedge family, and is very attractive.

Erianthus Ravennal is one of the most desirable species cultivated. It is quite hardy, and forms large clumps from which the stems rise to the height of ten to twelve feet, and are crowned with silvery plumes of twenty inches in length. A clump of this beautiful grass in full bloom, is an object of universal admiration. Its flowers are pure white, with a silvery lustre.

Gynerium argenteum (Pampas grass), is truly the "Queen of Ornamental Grasses." It must be seen to be appreciated. It is tender in the northern States, but its roots can be kept in boxes in the cellar during winter.

Panicum capilaceum is hardy, and very rich in foliage of rosy hue.

Pepragmites communis grows commonly along the banks of our northern rivers, but it is beautiful, and deserves a place among its foreign brethren. Its spikes of flowers are covered with long, white, silky hairs.

Stipa pennata (Feather grass), is very ornamental, the seeds vegetate slowly, and should be started under glass.

Trypsacum dactyloides is a very handsome and hardy grass.

Among the annual varieties I should select—

Agrostis retrafracta, an extremely graceful species; a great addition to bouquets and vases.

Agrostis Steveni, with beautiful, feathery panicles.

Avena sterilis (Animated Oats), with large drooping spikes of flowers.

Briza maxima (Quaking grass), very beautiful.

Briza geniculata, dwarf habit; very graceful.

Chloris radiata, a curious variety; very desirable.

Chloris truncata, silvery plumes.

Eleusine barcinonensis, a novelty with out-spreading plumes of flowers; lovely for house culture.

Hordeum jubatum (Squirrel-tail grass), lovely green and purplish plumes.

Lagurus ovatus (Hare's-tail grass), very pleasing.

Panicum variegatum, one of the most graceful and ornamental plants for baskets or vases.

Paspalum elegans, white flower.

CHAPTER XIV.

ORNAMENTAL FOLIAGED PLANTS.

"Oh ! who that has an eye to see,
A heart to feel, a tongue to bless,
Can ever undelighted be,
With nature's magic loveliness."

Variegated leaved plants are quite the fashion at this time, and are becoming more popular every year. They produce a fine effect when planted in oval or circular beds. The *furore* for these plants has produced a great variety; the whole world has been searched for rare specimens, and these have been hybridized, and greatly improved. A bed of them, well arranged as to color, is a most gorgeous sight, equal to any display of flowers.

A recent writer speaks of them thus:—

"Do not these curious plants, that among their leaves of light have no need of flowers, resemble those rare human plants that develop all the beauties of mind and character at an exceptionally early age, and rapidly ripen for the tomb? They do not live to bring forth the flowers and fruits of life's vigorous prime, and therefore God converts their foliage into leaves, crowns the initial stage with the glories of the final, and makes their very leaves beautiful. By the transfiguration of His grace, by the light that never was on sea or land, He adorns even their tender years with all the loveliness which in other cases comes only with full maturity."

A very pretty bed of Ornamental Plants can be sown from seed. In the center, plant the Striped-leaved Japanese Corn. A foot from it on all sides, sow seeds of the Cannas; soak the seeds in boiling water for an hour, and pour boiling water on the ground after the seeds are planted. If planted about the 10th of May, they will grow finely.

For the next row, sow Amaranthus melancholicus, and thin out the plants a foot apart. Next to these put the Silvery-leaved Cineraria maritima; and border the whole with Perilla Nankinensis. A row of white Candytuft could come after the Perilla, but it must be pulled up as soon as its flowers are past, or it will destroy the beauty of the bed. Such a bed could be obtained at a slight expense, not exceeding one dollar; while for a bed of Coleus—Achyranthus, Caladiums, Cineraria Acanthifolia, Alternantheras, Centaureas and Gnaphalium, sixty to seventy-five dollars is often paid. Of course, a bed of the latter description is far more *recherche* than one of the former; but only those whom Fortune has favored, can possess it; while you and I can delight our eyes daily with the bed of our own planting from seeds.

Coleus.

These plants take first rank among variegated plants. Coleus Verschaffeltii, with rich crimson leaves, veined with bronze and margined with green, was considered a rare wonder; but the Golden Coleus far surpass the early varieties. The American and English florists have been very successful with these lovely plants. They offer us this year:—

Beauty of Widmore, olive green, stained with pink, white edge.
Eclat, bronzy crimson, golden edge.
Acis, crimson, shaded carmine, golden edge.
Brilliant, bronzy crimson, broad golden margin.
Model, pinkish bronze, narrow golden border.
Princess Louise, reddish bronze, light yellow edge.
Golden Beauty, dark crimson, wavy and golden, fringed edge.
Setting Sun, rich bronze center, bright yellow edge.
Sunbeam, bronzy crimson, dark veins, yellow margin.
Unique, reddish crimson, deep golden border.
Of the older kinds the most noted are:—
Albert Victor, center purplish red, broad yellow margin.
Her Majesty, bronzy red center, greenish yellow margin.
Princess Royal, center reddish bronze, light yellow margin.
All of these make fine bedding-out plants; will grow in any rich.

sandy loam; they are very tender, the first frost blackens their beauty; and they require much heat in the winter. A slight chill is death to them. I had fine plants of several kinds last winter, but a cold night in December killed every one; green-house culture is needful for them.

Achyranthus.

These plants rank next to the Coleus in richness of coloring, and beauty of veining.

A. Acuminata has dark red leaves, marked with a salmon-red midrib, and light crimson under-surface. It contrasts charmingly with silvery-leaved plants.

Aureus Reticulatus has light green foliage, veined with yellow; stems crimson, very effective.

Achyranthus Lindenii is of a bushy growth, foliage rich, deep crimson.

All of these are very tender, but make good house plants during the winter.

Alternantheras.

These are dwarf plants from Brazil, with leaves tinted with crimson, pink, brown and green.

A. Amœna, crimson shaded to pink, and amber brown.
A. Amabilis, orange, crimson and dark green.
A. Leatifolia, foliage large, green, orange and crimson.
A. Versicolor, olive, crimson and chocolate.

These varieties are all used for edgings, and if they are closely cut, the fresh growth assumes most brilliant hues. They will not outlive our cold winters without protection.

Caladiums.

One of the most beautiful of the Ornamental Foliaged Plants for planting on the lawn, or as a center for oval or circular beds. They will grow five feet high, with immense leaves of a light green color, beautifully veined with various colors. They are bulbous roots, and must be taken up with the first frosts.

The bulbs should be kept in sand in a dry temperature, not below 50°.

Caladium Chatini, green ground, red and white spots.
Duc de Nassau, clear red leaf, beautifully shaded.
Emperor Napoleon, brilliant crimson, with rich blood-red ribs.
C. Houlletii, spotted and veined, with various shades of green.

Madame Houllet, pink spots towards the center, with white spots on the margin.

C. Sedeni, clouded, green and rose.

C. Splendens, rich crimson, shaded to a green margin.

C. Verschaffeltii, green ground, with pink spots.

The oldest and best known variety is the Caladium Esculeatum, the leaves are of immense size, often two feet long and six inches broad. It will thrive when the other tender varieties fail.

Begonias.

This class are remarkable for the diversity of their markings, and their rich crimson stems and edgings. Some of the leaves are of an immense size, with broad silvery zones and snowy spots, which contrast perfectly with the rich crimson-tinted, emerald-hued leaves.

Begonia Rex was the first variety; from it have sprung many rare kinds.

Begonia Hybrida Multiflora is valuable, especially for flowering during the winter months, blooming almost continually; has small ovate, glossy leaves, and a profusion of gracefully drooping racemes of rosy pink blossoms.

Cannas.

These are highly ornamental and effective; their broad, bright-hued leaves resemble those of the Banana; and their flowers are produced in racemes of scarlet, crimson, orange-red, and buff. They are tender, and must be removed to a dry cellar as soon as the frost comes. In spring start them in boxes, or in a warm climate, in the open border. They are grown from seed, as directed in this chapter; but one is not certain of procuring the best varieties. The bulbs can always be purchased at the florists at a small price.

Atropurpurea has fine dark leaves, with orange-scarlet flowers.

Insignis, leaves banded and rayed with purples; flowers reddish-orange.

Premices de Nice, large foliage, bright yellow flowers, spotted with salmon.

Rubra Superbissima, stalks crimson, leaves red, with a metallic shade, flowers clear orange-red.

Nigricans, leaves green with a dark bronze shade, flowers bright vermillion.

Ne plus ultra, leaves rich purple, flowers crimson-scarlet.

Musæfolia, foliage large and handsome.

Silver Foliage Plants

Are very desirable to plant in rows with the brightly hued Coleus, Achyranthus, etc.

Artemisia Stelleriana is a pretty dwarf plant.

Cineraria Acanthifolia has velvety white leaves, and is the most desirable of its kind.

Centaurea Gymnocarpa, very elegant, silvery leaves, with narrow, pointed lobes.

Centaurea Candidissima has snowy white leaves, with a frosted appearance.

Centaurea Clementei surpasses all its family in the elegance of its foliage. Its young leaves are like velvet, and, when fully developed, retain a silvery effect.

Gnaphalium Lanatum is of a dwarf, creeping habit, very desirable as a bordering.

Gnaphalium Tomentosum has long, narrow, silvery foliage.

Glaucium Corniculatum has long, velvety leaves, of a silvery white hue; leaves deeply pinnated; flowers of bell shape, orange yellow. It is a novelty introduced last season, and is much admired.

Achyrocline Saundersonii is dwarf and densely branched, with pure white leaves.

Coprosma Baneriana Variegata, a fine dwarf plant, with green oval leaves, flecked and veined with yellow; is a novelty from New Zealand.

Sinclairea Discolor has large, oval leaves, bright green on the upper side, but lined with a downy, snowy whiteness, producing a fine effect.

Wigandia Caraccasana is a stately, ornamental plant, whose large, bright green leaves are covered with hairy spines. Its flowers are of rich purple, borne on a large spike.

Fittonia Argyroneura is lovely for vases, hanging baskets, or ferneries. Its leaves are of bright green, netted with pearly white veins.

Acorus Gramineus Variegata is also desirable for baskets, etc. Its narrow, grass-like leaves are margined with bright yellow.

Panicum Variegatum is also a grass, striped with white and rose; will grow two or three feet in a season; is very elegant.

Abutilon Thompsonii is a prettily variegated shrub, with leaves marbled with yellow.

Sedum Carneum Variegatum is of dwarf growth, with lance-shaped green leaves, margined with white. Beautiful for rock work, but will not endure the winter of the Northern States.

I cannot close a chapter on Variegated Plants, without mention of the

Golden Bronze and the Silver Margined Geraniums.

This class form most beautiful groups or beds, very effective either on the lawn or in the garden.

Mrs. Pollock is one of the best known of these varieties, but Lady Cullum surpasses it in the beauty of its zone.

Sir Robert Napier is said to possess the handsomest coloring of all. Its zone is deeply indented with brilliant scarlet; flowers flesh colored.

Sophie Dumaresque has a dark crimson zone, with broad yellow margin.

Black Prince, dark bronze zone, on a yellow ground.

Beauty of Oulton, broad yellow leaf, with a wide bronze zone.

Bronze Queen, yellowish bronze, with a dark chocolate zone; contrasts perfectly with the silver-edged varieties.

Southern Belle, golden yellow ground, brilliant crimson zone.

E. G. Henderson, light yellow ground, fine dark bronzy zone.

Beauty of Calderdale, reddish brown zone on a golden green ground.

Crystal Palace Gem, golden margin, green center.

Perilla, broad dark zone.

Queen Victoria, rich maroon zone, golden yellow margin.

Silver Margined Geraniums.

Cherub, silver margined, carmine zone, dwarf.

Burning Bush, sulphur white, with bronze zone of rosy crimson tint.

Beauty of Guestwick, zone bronze and rosy carmine, creamy white margin.

Castlemilk, pea-green center, well defined white edge, the whitest of its class.

Countess of Warwick, broad white margin, zone dark bronze, banded with pink.

May Queen, fine broad silver edge.

Kenilworth, white margin, rich crimson zone.

Mt. of Snow, pure white, broad edge.

Rainbow, silvery white margin, red zone.

Snow Storm. fine white edge.

Italia Unita, silver edge, dark zone shaded to carmine.
Little Pet. pink zone, silver edge.
Snow Drop, fine silvery white edge.
Perfection, broad white margin, fine.

Variegated Ivy-Leaved Geraniums.

These flowers are very lovely, from their drooping growth, for vases, rustic baskets and rock work. They grow readily from slips, are quite tender, and must be housed during the winter months.

L'Elegante has deep pea-green leaves, with a clear white margin running into pink. Its flowers are pure white, borne in large clusters. It is unsurpassed for ornamental purposes, where vines are required.

Duke of Edinburgh is beautifully variegated, and of very vigorous growth.

Holly Wreath has leaves of deep green, with a creamy margin, white flowers.

Peltatum Floribunda, leaves bright glossy green, flowers of a rosy pink.

Fairy Bells, rich green leaves, flowers a light blush.

Elegans, bright rich foliage, mauve colored flowers.

All these Variegated Geraniums grow readily from cuttings, and will bloom in almost any common garden soil. They show their bright markings at better advantage if located so that they are shaded from the heat of the noonday sun. Planted together, *en masse*, they produce a gorgeous effect. All of them have brilliant colored flowers, but they are not as large and handsome as those of the Zonale tribe. If planted on a graduated mound, with a tall Zonale or Double Geranium for the apex, they show in perfect contrast. They require watering at night, if the season is hot and dry. They can be wintered in a warm window, or placed in sandy soil, in boxes, and kept in a frost-proof cellar.

Of course the leaves will fall, but the roots will remain alive, and will not require water more than once or twice all winter, unless they are kept in a warm place near the furnace fire; but this is not a good location for them; far better to keep them in a cool, dark cellar, where vegetation can sleep quietly.

CHAPTER XV.

Spring Flowering Bulbs.

"Odors of spring, my senses ye charm!
Methinks with purpose soft ye come,
To tell of brighter hours;
Of May's blue skies, abundant bloom,
And sunny gales and showers."

In October and November we must plant the Spring Flowering Bulbs, which are the first flowers in the spring that gladden our eyes. As soon as the sun's rays have strength enough to pierce the stony ground, they send up their leaves closely sheathed together to withstand the icy touch of the north wind. With the first sweet whistle of the robin, and the clear treble notes of the blue bird, they stand ready to burst forth into gorgeous splendor. The pearly white Snowdrop, white as the snow-drift which has nourished her buds, is the pale leader of the gloriously clad procession which follows the spring's footsteps.

Clusters of these roots can be planted among the grass nearest the house, and early in March and April they will appear in full bloom. They will grow in any soil; but will run out if new homes are not provided for them every three or four years. They multiply rapidly. The great Snowdrop is double the size of the common kind, but does not blossom so early. The small sorts can be planted an inch apart and two inches deep, but the larger kinds should be planted five inches asunder, and four inches in depth.

The Crocus

Comes next in order, clothed in purple, yellow and white, lilac and blue; striped and plain; cloth of gold and cloth of silver. They are of easy culture, and increase rapidly by offsets; they can remain in the ground three years, but may be taken up every year, when their leaves have become yellow. October is the best season for replanting them, but November will do in warm climates. They should be planted two inches deep, and an inch or two apart. The new varieties are raised from seed. These bulbs are perfectly hardy, but will come forward better in the spring, if the ground is covered with a bed of leaves or evergreen boughs.

Among the new varieties are:—
Albion, blue, striped with white.
Caroline Chisholm, purest white.
Cloth of Gold, yellow, striped with black.
Cloth of Silver, white, striped with purple.
David Rizzio, dark purple.
Elise, light shaded.
Ivanhoe, blue and white.
Ne plus ultra, blue bordered.
Miss Nightingale, light striped.
Queen Victoria, pure white.
Scotch, yellow, with purple stripes.
Sir Walter Scott, pencilled lilac.
Van Speyk, violet striped.

The Hyacinth.

This plant, though a native of the desert, has been domesticated for many centuries, and is aptly styled the "Domestic Flower," for it is dearly loved in many homes.

Haarlem is the great focus of bulbous cultivation; its soil consists of light vegetable mould mixed with sand, and under this is a substrata of sand which drains off the heavy spring rains. Florists of other countries have imitated this soil, thereby producing as fine bulbs as can be raised in Holland.

All new varieties are raised from seeds, but much care and patience are required, and often not more than six fine flowers will be found in a thousand seedlings; so it is the best to content ourselves with raising them from the bulbs, which multiply rapidly by offsets, which should be planted out by themselves, in a dry, sunny location; if they attempt to flower the first spring, pick off the buds, for the root needs all its strength; but the next spring they will flower well, and after that can be treated like grown-up bulbs.

If the beds in which the Hyacinths and other bulbs have flowered are needed before the roots have fully matured, they can be taken up and laid in ridges, covering the roots with sandy earth, but leaving the stems and leaves fully exposed to the air; they will soon decay, and the bulbs will swell to full maturity. If the ground is not required for other plants, the beds can remain for two or three years undisturbed, but larger flowers are produced by yearly transplantings. The seed-pods should be broken off before they have had time to develop, as ripening the seed would tend to exhaust the strength of the bulb, but the leaves are needful to prepare the pulp for maturing the bulb for another season; therefore they must not be cut off until they are wholly dried up. When quite dry, separate the offsets, and place by themselves in paper bags or boxes, and keep in a dark, dry closet, until time to replant them. Their roots will strike through a mellow soil, from ten to even twelve inches; therefore to raise the finest blossoms, the soil should be removed at least one foot in depth, and the earth well broken up; then spread over it a layer of three or four inches of leaf mould, well mixed with sand, and fill up with a compost of one-third well-rotted cow manure, and two-thirds sandy loam, well mingled, If the soil under the pine trees of the woods can be obtained, you will make your bulbs blossom in perfection; it is a dark, sandy loam, excellently fitted for flowering all bulbs. Scouring sand, which can be found in nearly every kitchen, is very useful in planting bulbs; put a table-spoonful into each hole, and set the bulb upon it. Plant in concentric circles, straight rows, or clusters, and cover the largest sized bulbs, at least three to four inches. A liberal top dressing of sand will draw the sun's rays early in the season. As soon as the ground freezes hard, cover the beds with four or five inches of straw, leaves, or coarse stable litter; but don't cover them too early, else the ground mouse may burrow in the warm bed, and feed upon your bulbs.

As soon as the green sheathed leaves appear, remove part of the covering, and press the earth tightly around the bulbs, else they will crack the earth, and let the chilling winds into the roots. In ten days or a fortnight, if the weather is warm, remove all the coverings.

The florists' catalogues are issued every autumn, and offer us a large variety of roots with high-sounding names. In the selection of bulbs, choose those that are compact, solid, and firm at the base of the root.

The double varieties are usually the most desirable for out-door culture, and they will often cover at least half of the stem with lovely bells, forming a compact cone, terminated at the top by an upright flower. The single varieties are better for window gardening, and some of them are indispensable to every collection.

A bed of Hyacinths in full bloom is a glory and a joy, but in planting them due deference must be paid to their height, and time of blooming, or the whole effect may be spoiled; and some catalogues properly mention, not only the names, but the seasons and height of the flowers.

A select list of double and single varieties:—

Double, Dark and Light Blue.

Albion, late, low.
King of Wurtemburg, early, tall, very fine
A la Mode, early, low, a perfect blue.
Pasquin, early, tall, a light blue.
Globe Terrestre, late, low, perfect flower.
Laurens Coster, low, early.
Koning Ascingaris, tall, early.
Bloksberg, late, low.
Lord Raglan, low, early.
Richard Steele, low, early.

Single, Blue of all shades,

L'Amie de Cœur, tall, early, very dark.
L'Unique, tall, early, rich purplish blue.
Bleu Mourant, late, low, deep blue.
Charles Dickens, tall, early, perfect flower.
Porcelaine Scepter, low, early, light blue.
La Peyrouse, low, early, porcelaine blue.

Double, White.

Duc de Berry, late, tall.
Duchess of Bedford, late, low.
La Deese, late, low.
La Virginitie, low, early.
Virgo, tall, early.
Lord Anson low, early.

Single, White.

Alba Superbissima, low, early.
Bella Donna, late, low.

Blanchard, tall, early.
La Candeur, low, early.
Queen Victoria, low, early.
Queen of the Netherlands, tall, early.

Double, Red and Rose.

Belle Marie, late, tall.
Bouquet Constant, low, early.
La Gaiete, low, early.
Mars, late, low.
Sir Thomas Grey, late, low.
Czar Nicholas, low, early.
Lord Wellington, low, early, fine.
Perruque Royale, late, tall.

Single, Red and Rose.

Belle Corrinne, low, early.
Madame Hodson, tall, early.
Robert Steiger, tall, early.
Princess Victoria, late, low.
Jenny Lind, low, early.
Duchess of Richmond, tall, early.

Double, Yellow.

Bouquet d'Orange, low, early.
Crœsus, late, low.
Jaune Supreme, tall, early.
La Grandeur, late, low.
Van Spek, tall, early.

Single, Yellow.

Alida Jacobea, low, early.
Anna Carolina, late, low.
Fleur d'Or, low, early.
Koning Van Holland, low, early.
La Pluie d'Or, tall, early.
Prit Hein, low, early.
Rhinosceros, tall, early.

The Tulip.

This bulbous plant has been aptly styed "The Fop of Flowers," for it is the most gorgeous of all the spring flowers, and its variety of colors, most delicately blended, are almost beyond the power of imagination.

Their culture is so simple, that no one can well afford to be without a bed of them, for an early display of gorgeous bloom.

They are natives of Persia, and the name is derived from *tulipan*, a turban, the calyx of the flower resembling that Eastern head-dress. The Turks first cultivated them, and from thence they were sent to Vienna. At first they were supposed to be eatable, like onions, but were found unpalatable; then they were preserved in sugar, but their taste was not improved, so they were thrown out upon a refuse heap as worthless trash; here they bloomed, and thus revealed the beauty of the flower.

Conrad Gesner, the Swiss botanist, first saw the flower in 1559, and described it scientifically. Many years afterwards, Linnæus gave the flower the specific name of Gesneriana, in honor of Gesner.

Linnæus styles bulbs, "The hybernacle, or winter lodge, of the young plants." Darwin says, "These bulbs in every respect resemble buds, except in their being produced under ground, and include the leaves and flowers in minature which are to be expanded in the ensuing spring. By cautiously cutting in winter through the concentric coats of a Tulip root, longitudinally from the top to the base, and taking them off successively, the whole flower of the next summer's Tulip is beautifully seen by the naked eye, with its petals, pistils, and stamens. The flowers exist in other bulbs in the same manner, but their individual flowers being of less size, they are not so easily dissected, or so conspicuous to the naked eye. The poet thus describes the bulb:—

> "Quick flies fair Tulipa the loud alarms,
> And folds her infant closer in her arms;
> In some lone cave's secure pavilion lies,
> And waits the courtship of serener skies."

In the first half of the 17th century the historical episode of the tulipomania occurred. It commenced in Holland, thence spread to France, and England would have felt its influence had she not been fully occupied with the more sanguinary mania of civil war. The almost incredible extravagances of this mania are usually laid to the Dutch; but this is erroneous. As well attribute the deeds of reckless stock speculators in railways, to the scientific engineers who planned and constructed them.

The high esteem in which the Dutch held the flower, doubtless sowed the seeds of the disease; but the immense prices given for single roots, had no reference to their floral value. It was the love of gambling, and not the love of flowers, which created them. Speculators bought or sold tulip roots at a certain price, to be delivered at a specified time, just as the frequenters of the stock exchange speculate by *time bargains* in stock. Thus the tulip king of the era would possess himself of a certain variety of Tulip, and then offer to purchase more; other dealers, supposing they could procure them easily, would undertake to deliver a certain quantity at such a time, at an agreed price; that variety would rise in value, and so the artful speculator could obtain almost any price he pleased for his roots, purchased at a low price.

"Bulls," "bears," "ducks," "gulls" and other like animals, well known to those who frequent the stock markets, are not a modern invention; but centuries ago existed in Holland and France. The Dutch amateurs loved their Tulip roots as they loved their own houses and lands, and Crabbe tells us that:—

> "With all his phlegm, it broke a Dutchman's heart,
> At a vast price, with one loved root to part."

Some individuals gave all they possessed for the coveted bulbs, and we read that one root was exchanged for four fat oxen.

In England, as late as 1835, a root named "Fanny Kemble" sold at auction for $225.

Tulips do not bloom quickly from the seed; five years at least must elapse before "the bright, consummate flower" appears, and its bloom is usually a *self*, or mere ground color, and is termed a breeder; but in a few years the calyx will become variegated, and it is termed *broken*; so when a really choice variety is produced, its annual offsets is its only means of propagation, and it must command a high price for some years.

The late variety of Tulip mostly cultivated is T. Gesneriana, and is divided into three classes, viz.:—roses, byblomens, and bizarres. The "roses" are marked with cherry, scarlet, pink and crimson stripes or veins, on a white ground. They are usually eighteen inches high, and their cups are large and well formed. The "byblomens" are marked with black, lilac or purple, on a white ground; and the "bizarres" are feathered with purple, pink, cherry, scarlet, etc., on a yellow ground.

These classes are still divided into flamed and feathered. A Tulip has neither corolla or petal, but a calyx of colored sepals. A feathered Tulip has a dark colored edge, growing lighter toward the margin.

Those of our readers who have never seen a bed of these Tulips cannot even imagine the brilliancy of their colorings and gorgeous featherings. When planted in diamonds, ovals, stars or circles, on a well kept lawn, the effect is splendid!

The "Duc Van Thol" varieties are a very early kind, blossoming in temperate climates early in March. They are dwarfs, their stems not over six inches high, and they are excellent for winter flowering in window gardens. There are white, yellow, scarlet, red, rose and striped varieties, and small beds of them scattered over a lawn, present at a distance the appearance of brilliant butterflies hovering over the grass. They are perfectly hardy, but will flower more plentifully if taken up every spring, when the leaves have decayed.

The "Tournesol" species come into bloom next to the "Van Thols," and are double and only in two kinds; the red and yellow, and the clear, pure yellow. In mixed beds they are very gorgeous.

The Double Tulips gain in favor yearly; their flowers are very brilliant and large.

Crown of Roses is of the richest rose color
Belle Alliance, white, striped, and feathered with violet.
Gloria Mundi, delicate primrose, striped with crimson.
La Candeur, of the purest white and perfect shape.
Poupre Agreable, white and violet, late.
Marriage de ma Fille, pure white, striped with cerise, late.
Pæony Gold, yellow, beautifully shaded, late.
Lord Wellington, blue, very showy, late.
Amsterdam, brown and red, curiously blended, late.

The Parrot Tulips are the most curious and unique of all the varieties. The flowers are magnificently striped and feathered, with many colors, most picturesquely mingled, while the edges of the sepals are fringed like fretted lace work. They are very desirable for groups and clumps, and, if planted around low evergreens, will stand out finely against the dark, green background.

The most distinct varieties are:—
Constantinople, a bright yellow and red.
Glorieuse, a brilliant scarlet.

Markgraf, striped, red and yellow.
Monstre Rouge, large, crimson.
Belle Jaune, large yellow, feathered with red and green.

Cultivation of the Tulip.

Fresh, sandy loam, such as is obtained from upland pastures, is the best soil. Remove the sods from sheep or cow pastures, and take the virgin soil. The late blooming Tulips should be planted four inches in depth; the "Van Thols," etc., from two to three inches, according to their size, and their roots will strike down from five to six inches. Good garden soil, mixed with cow manure, two years-old, and a plentiful sprinkling of sand, will grow them to advantage. Never put fresh barnyard compost near them; it will burn up the bulbs.

They should be planted in November, and be firmly set in the soil, six inches apart for the tall varieties, and four inches for the "Van Thols." Sprinkle sand, as directed for Hyacinths, into each hole; this will keep the bulbs from rotting at the base. After the ground freezes, cover with straw, or leaves, for the freezing and thawing of the ground injures the blooms of the next spring.

When the leaves fall, cut off the stems, and when the leaves are dried up the bulbs can be removed, the offsets separated, and treated just like Hyacinths.

In selecting the bulbs, choose those that are solid, a little pointed, and the skin entire.

These flowers will richly repay the little care expended upon them, and I especially desire to call the attention of lady florists to their merits.

As I write this chapter, I feast my eyes on a small bed of "Van Thols" that are perfectly gorgeous, and attract the attention of every passer-by. The cold north wind whistles around the windows, and bends the brilliant calyx of their blooms, but does not mar their beauty. By their side sweet Hyacinths bloom, and they are all the flowers which my garden can boast in this young spring-time.

The Daffodils.

These are hardy bulbs, which are common in old-fashioned gardens, and our grandmothers loved to cherish them. They will bloom in out-of-the-way places for years and years, and ask no care or attention. The flowers are of a brilliant yellow.

The Jonquils.

Their creamy, rose-tipped chalices are always lovely, and the double varieties are fair and white as roses; but some of them lack the fragrance of their sister bulbs.

The Narcissus.

This is an extensive family which grows freely in any good garden loam. The Daffodil and Jonquil belong to the family, and there are many varieties of the Polyanthus Narcissus, which are the most lovely bulbs of the class. Their flowers are formed in clusters of six to twelve flowers on a single stem, and of every shade from purest white to deepest orange. The cup of the white varieties is always yellow, and of the yellow, a deep orange. These bulbs flower finely in the window garden, and three or four bulbs can be grown in a small pot. The Double Narcissus is very desirable for its perfect flower and spicy fragrance. They all require the same treatment as Hyacinths, and should be planted four inches deep, and set out in clumps, ten inches apart.

Anemones.

These are very lovely bulbs; their colors are gorgeous, and the markings, belts and stripes very charming. Double and single are both beautiful. The bulbs are tender in our north countries, and can be kept in the house until spring, in a dry, cool place, and set out as soon as the ground is well thawed. In mild climates they can be planted in October or November. They bloom after the earlier bulbs are gone, and their flowers last a long time. When the leaves turn yellow, take up the roots, dry in the shade, and pack away in sand until autumn.

The Lily of the Valley

Must not be forgotten among Spring Flowering Bulbs, though her roots partake more of the nature of small, thin tubers. She hangs her pearly bells like so many fragrant censers, and is ever welcome and ever lovely —a true home flower, sanctified to many hearts by both festive and funeral occasions. No garden is complete without a bed of them!

There are both double and single varieties, but the latter are the most common. These sweet flowers require no care, will bloom for years in the same bed, and throw out their pure white tuberous roots far into the pathways. They love the shade, and flourish best in an out-of-the-way corner, where the soil is moist and rich. Are perfectly hardy, requiring no protection in the coldest winter. There is no bulb that flourishes so perfectly under neglect; and no flower which is more perfect in form and fragrance.

The Ranunculus.

There are two kinds of these bulbs—the Double Persian, and the Turban; they form a fine contrast when planted together. They require a rich soil, at least a foot and a half in depth of friable, rich earth; that taken from a marshy wood—deep and dark, and mixed with very old decomposed manure—is the best for them. They need to be frequently watered; drought will kill their blossoms, and they are too tender to endure the cold of northern winters, but must be kept in dry sand, and planted out three inches deep, early in the spring. The hot sun will fade out their bright colors, so it is best to plant them in the shade.

Ixias, Scillas, Irises, Colchicums and Crown Imperials are all good border plants, and add variety to a bed of bulbous roots.

Generally, any well-drained garden soil will answer for them; if clay, a good sprinkling of sand, and a top dressing of well decayed manure will make them bloom more freely.

CHAPTER XVI.

BULBS FOR SUMMER FLOWERING.

"'Look at the Lilies, how they grow!'
'Twas thus the Saviour said, that we,
E'en in the simplest flowers that blow,
God's ever watchful care might see.

Shall He who paints the Lily's leaf,
Who gives the Rose its scented breath,
Love all His works, except the chief,
And leave His image, man, to death?"

The Japan Lilies.

Bulbs that can be preserved in the house in a dry state during the winter, and planted in the ground in the spring, or those which live out during the winter and bloom in the house, are called Summer Bulbs.

To this class belong the Japan Lilies, Gladiolus, Dahlias, Tuberoses, Tigridias, Amaryllis formosissima, Valotta purpurea superba, and Tritomas.

These flowers are of very easy cultivation, and contribute largely to the beauty of the garden; their magnificent bloom well repaying the little attention they require. The peculiar nature of a bulb is not generally well understood; it really partakes more of the properties of a seed, for, when in the act of vegetating it sends down into the soil roots, and into the air a living stem, and the matter contained in the bulb decomposes and nourishes the young plant, while the seed decays in giving birth to the plant; but the bulb is renewed, and from the roots another bulb is composed which appears to be the same one planted, yet it is its offspring, and the offsets or young bulbs are its suckers, and are distinct from the parent bulb. Thus like the myth of the Phenix springing from the ashes of the parent bulb, the offspring is formed. This formation is readily seen in the Gladiolus and the Crocus.

The rarely beautiful Lilies which have been imported from Japan are great additions to the list of summer flowers. They are shaped like the old-fashioned Tiger Lily, always seen in old gardens, but entirely surpass it in the beauty of their coloring.

They were first treated as "stove plants," and did not show forth their glories, but now they will survive the coldest northern winter with a slight covering of leaves, and have proved themselves indispensable.

They grow readily in any good soil, but like all other flowers, will repay their cultivator if supplied with a rich, loamy soil, mixed with sandy peat; this is their native soil, and they will produce many more flowers upon one stalk if attention is paid to their wants. They require much moisture when in flower, and if the season is very hot and dry, will bloom much longer if mulched with moist manure.

We are indebted to the enterprising and scientific traveler, Dr. Siebold, for the introduction of the Japan Lilies to our gardens.

Lilium speciosum has been thus described:—"The clear, deep rose-color of its petals are all rugged with rubies and garnets, sparkling with crystal points. Indeed, the diamond bouquets, the Queen of Spain's jewels, and even the far-famed Koh-i-noor itself, must pale their ineffectual fires, when compared with this gorgeous flower. The jeweler who wishes to produce a most exquisitely tasteful, as well as dazzling and brilliant ornament, should take one of these Lilies as his model."

Lilium lancifolium album has pure white flowers; sometimes the lower part of the petals are washed with violet.

Lilium lancifolium punctatum has flowers of a flesh color, with spots of delicate rose.

Lilium lancifolium rubrum possesses very large flowers of rose-color, suffused with carmine, and purplish colored papilla.

Lilium longiflorum is a very beautiful species, growing nearly two feet high, and producing from one to five flowers, according to the size of the bulb; the flowers are of a pure, waxy white, trumpet shaped, and from six to eight inches long. It blooms early in July, while the above-named varieties do not bloom until August.

Lilium eximium is another handsome variety, resembling L. longiflorum, but the flowers are larger and their color is of a sating whiteness.

Lilium Brownii possesses many of the characteristics of the two preceding, but the outside of the flower is striped with deep brownish-violet lines.

All these Lilies will grow and blossom luxuriantly for several weeks. They increase rapidly by small bulbs below the soil, and it is well to remove them every autumn, and plant them separately. Thus treated, they will often bloom the second season. The small bulbs should be planted in a light, sandy soil, and covered two inches deep. The soil should not be made too rich with manure, as it tends to rot the bulbs. A Double Japan Lily has been produced, but as yet the bulbs are very rare and high priced.

And Mr. Fortune has introduced from China, Lilium tigrinum Fortunei, which is remarkable for its vigorous growth, and its immense cluster of flowers which branch out in three successive series from the main stem, thus prolonging its season of bloom.

Another novelty is Lilium tigrinum splendens, introduced by M. Van Houtte, which resembles the Fortunei in many respects, but differs from it in color, and has more prominent spots on the perianth. Both of them are considered gorgeous additions to the family of bulbous plants.

Lilium auratum is styled the "Queen of the Japanese Lilies." To its perfect form and rare coloring, it adds the most delicious fragrance. Its blossoms are very large, and each petal is decorated with a golden band running through its center. It is perfectly hardy, and often produces from fifteen to twenty-five blossoms on a single stalk. Good flowering bulbs are now held at a low price. It flowers in August, but by planting in pots its time of blossoming can be forestalled. Like the other Lilies, it delights in a sandy loam. The Japan Lilies make fine lawn plants. If planted in a circular bed, with the tallest in the center, the effect is very pleasing.

The Gladiolus.

The Gladiolus has become the chief favorite among its class. Its name is derived from its sword-shaped leaves; it possesses upwards of sixty species, divided by hybridization into an immense number of varieties. In nearly all the species the flowers retain the same form, but they differ in colorings and markings. These bulbs are mostly natives of Cape of Good Hope, Madagascar and Southern Africa. They will not survive our northern climate, and must always be kept in a cool, dry place during the winter.

In their native land, they bloom during the wet season, which shows us that they require a good supply of moisture to bloom in perfection in our dry, hot summers.

These flowers were not much known until 1795, when the Cape Colony was ceded to England, and her botanists and collectors of rare plants seized upon them with delight. Since then they have become "Florists' Flowers," and their successful hybridizations have greatly increased their beauty and colorings.

To grow the bulbs in perfection, they should be planted in a sandy loam, enriched with leaf mould and peat. A mixture of one-half loam, one-quarter peat, and one-quarter leaf mould will suit them perfectly.

They may be planted in the open air during April or May.

If strong manures are used in the soil, it causes the colors of the flowers to run into each other, and gives them a muddy appearance. The bulbs can be planted in groups or singly. Groups of three or five are the most usual way of planting them. They should be set from two to four inches deep, according to the size of the bulbs. As they grow up, they should be tied to a light stake, from three to four feet long.

When the frost has killed the leaves, dig up the bulbs, dry them in the sun, cut off the leaves an inch from the stem, and put the bulbs in a paper bag. Kept in a frost-proof cellar, they will retain all their life. From one bulb, two or three bulbs will spring; they increase rapidly, and can be purchased cheaply.

The high prices in the catalogues are no criterion of their beauty, but only mark them as "novelties."

Many bulbs are held at four dollars a root, but that shows their scarcity.

Low priced varieties will often please us quite as well, and are not surpassed by the colors of the "novelties."

Among the most beautiful of the Gladiolus, are:—

Belle Gabrielle, a perfectly shaped flower, fine lilac-colored rose, marked with a bright rose-color.

Charles Dickens, delicate rose, tinted with chamois, striped with a rosy carmine.

Comte de Morny, rosy scarlet flecked with rich crimson, lower petals shaded with crimson.

Dr. Lindley, very large flower of perfect shape, rose-color petals of a brighter shade, feathered with cherry-color; very showy.

Lady Franklin, white, slightly tinged with rose, striped and blazed with carminate rose.

La Français, flower pure white, and very large, with small bluish violet blotches; very fine.

Moliere, flower very large; a bright cherry-red with large, pure white stains.

Mozart, bright rose, tinted with violet, blazed with dark carmine, with pure white stains; a very beautiful variety.

Roi Leopold, bright rose, tinged with orange, and stained with white.

Stephenson, large flower, cherry-colored, striped with white lines; splendid spike of flowers.

Stella, perfect shaped flower, white ground, slightly tinged with yellow and rose; very brilliant and showy.

Sir Walter Scott, very bright rose-color on a white ground, striped with carmine; very fine.

Vicomtesse de Belleval, delicate blush, stained with violet.

Good varieties can be purchased from $1.50 to $2.00 per dozen.

Gladioli show to good advantage if planted around rose bushes, or among herbaceous perennials. They bloom late in the season, when most of these flowers are past, and if well trained to stakes, which should be set when the flower is planted, they will produce a charming effect. They make very nice house plants for window gardens; six or eight bulbs can be grown in a twelve-inch pot, and each kind tied to a thin stake. They will bloom finely. If the stalks are cut off for vases or bouquets, they will continue to bloom for a week or two, sending forth fresh flowers daily.

There is no bulbous root which gives a greater variety of colors in its flowers, or better repays the care and attention bestowed upon it. All lovers of flowers must cultivate a few of these desirable bulbs.

The Dahlia.

The great variety and beauty of its blossoms, and their profusion in the later summer and autumn, when many of our handsomest flowers are gone, make it well worthy of good culture. The Dahlia is a native of Mexico, and was found by Baron Humboldt growing on the elevated, sandy plains of Mexico, five thousand feet above the level of the sea.

He gatnered the seeds and sent them to the Abbe Cavanilles, Professor of Botany at the Royal Garden of Madrid, who succeeded in flowering a plant in October, 1789, to which he gave the name of Dahlia pinnata, in honor of Dahl, a Swedish botanist, a pupil of Linnæus. Objections were made to this name because it resembled Dalea, a name given to an entirely different plant, in honor of Dale, an Englishman. Professor Wildenow, in his "Species Plantarum," calls it Georgina, after Georgi, a Russian botanist. De Candolle and other eminent writers adopted that title; but the original name was the favorite, and still exists. In 1790, the Marchioness of Bute received some seeds from Spain, which flowered finely, but not knowing how to treat the tubers in the winter, the plants were lost. In 1804, Lady Holland sent seeds to M. Buonainti, a practical gardner and skillful botanist; he cultivated them successfully, and from those seeds almost all the various kinds of Dahlias have sprung.

De Candolle obtained seeds, and in 1810 he describes only five varieties of Variabilis, and three of Frustranea; but he had no double flower.

The first double Dahlia was sent from Stuttgard to Mons. Von Otto, who raised one similar, in the Royal Garden at Berlin, in 1809. He labored patiently to improve the varieties, and by 1816 had three more double flowers; but not until 1820 could he show six double flowering kinds. Now they are counted by the hundreds and thousands; and it would seem as if there were no limits to the improvement of it. Mr. Paxton asks, "Who would have supposed, that from one comparatively insignificant plant, such endless, innumerable, beautiful varieties could have been produced; and what may we not anticipate? It is not unreasonable to expect still a greater improvement. May we not have combinations of those clear, rich, and exquisitely beautiful colors for which the Tulip has been so long admired? Perhaps, ere long, our fancy may be gratified by seeing Dahlias with the shades of black and white associated in the same flower; and the popular taste may be also gratified with globular shaped flowers."

A blue Dahlia was the *ne plus ultra* for which the florists strove, and many watered their young seedlings with an infusion of indigo, hoping thereby to give the desired cerulean hue.

Mons. de Candolle considers yellow and blue to be the fundamental types of colors in flowers, and that they are antagonistic, i. e., mutually exclude each other; the blue flowers can by cultivation be changed into all shades of red, purple and white, while the yellow will pass into the same shades, but never into blue. For many years the Dahlia showed only the shades of purple and crimson, and it was not believed that any other color could be produced. A pure white flower at length was produced, and caused a great sensation; and the yellow was greeted with much delight. The growing of Dahlias was a passion in England and the United States, twenty years ago; and new varieties were much sought for. Large sums of money were paid for them.

The Liliputian or Pompone Dahlias are very lovely for bouquets and vases. The flowers are of the desired globular shape, and each petal is perfectly cupped and tinted. They grow about eighteen inches to two feet high, and are desirable for the smallest garden. Some of the flowers are no larger than a Ranunculus; the plant is perfectly covered with buds and flowers that produce a charming effect.

Dahlias will grow in almost any kind of soil, excepting wet, heavy clay loam; but a moderately rich, light loam is the best. A clear, open location, well exposed to the sun, is indispensable for the finest blooms. They grow finely on the southwestern side of a fence, making a hedge of unsurpassed beauty. The plants should be set three feet apart; if grown *en masse*, they should have as much room as that, and they will grow so bushy, that at a little distance, they will appear closely grouped. As borderings on each side of a walk, they show to great advantage, and can be planted once in two and a half feet.

Dahlias can be trained by pegging down the tender shoots, so that they will cover a bed; the branches must be pegged down as the plants grow, until the bed is entirely covered, and will present an uniform mass of flowers and foliage. Plants for this purpose should be set only two feet apart. Some train them in the espalier form, by allowing three or four stems to grow from each root, laying them diagonally on both sides, and filling up the center with the lateral shoots.

These flowers are propagated by seeds, division of the tubers, and by cuttings. Few, but experienced florists, succeed in growing them in the last-named manner, but all of us can raise them from the two former. It is no more work to grow a Dahlia than a potato.

Keeping Dahlias through the Winter.

The tubers need not be dug up until just before the ground freezes; then remove them to a dry out-house for a day or two to dry off. Don't break the tubers apart, but cut the stem down to within a few inches of them, and use it as a handle by which to lift them. All the flowering stems of another season are situated on or near the point of junction between the tubers and the stem. When they are so dried that the soil will all shake off, pack them in barrels or boxes and fill up with sand that has been dried in the sun especially for them. If you put them in damp sand they will decay. After they are carefully packed, put them in a dry cellar—frost-proof, and they will come out in March and April fresh and vigorous. In planting them, it is considered best to set out the cluster of tubers, and after the shoots have sprouted two or three inches, to separate them, leaving two shoots to a tuber. When planted out into the border, put the root at least three inches under ground, and water carefully, shading from the sun for two or three days. A stake must be inserted close by the stem when the tuber is planted, and as the shoots advance, tie them to it. If placed there after the plant is growing, you may injure the roots.

It is from seeds alone that new varieties spring. They should be sown early in the spring, in shallow boxes in a window or hot-bed, in a rich, light soil, with a good sprinkling of sand; as soon as the third and fourth leaves are well developed, plant them in two-inch pots, or in boxes three inches apart; shade them from the light for two days or so, as the seedlings are very tender. They can be planted into the border when all danger of frost is past; and if the soil is enriched with well-rotted cow-manure, the blooms will be finer. Until the buds show their coloring, there is no way of ascertaining it with certainty, though plants with pure green stems will usually produce white flowers, those with reddish-brown stems the darkest colored flowers, and those with light brown stems, pale or blush-colored flowers. Such plants as are not handsome should be pulled up, as soon as the flowers have fully shown their character; and give more room for the beautiful ones to grow in.

If the finest blooms are desired, the side branches should all be pinched off, and only the three or four strongest shoots allowed to grow, and on these the buds must be thinned out, leaving only three or four to come to perfection. The hot sun is injurious to the more delicate shades, and careful cultivators suspend an oiled paper, to protect their rare plants from it, also from heavy, drenching rains.

Soapsuds make an excellent fertilizer, and it is well to give the roots a thorough drenching with it, at least once a week. Much of the success in growing fine Dahlias depends upon training them carefully, and

fastening the shoots with soft yarn to the stake every few days. By protecting from the first frosts, the blossoms may be prolonged late into the autumn, after the death of most flowers of the garden, and if gathered and kept in fresh water, the flowers will last a fortnight, or even longer.
A select list of varieties:—

America, raised by Mr. Gerhard Schmitz, of Philadelphia, who has been very successful in producing fine varieties; white ground, striped and splashed with rosy-crimson, perfect globular shade, and cupped petals. Received first prize from Pennsylvania Horticultural Society.

Amazon, scarlet margins, yellow center.
Alba multiflora, pure white.
Ali Baba, deep scarlet.
Amorette, light rose, edged with lilac.
Antiope, buff, shaded with carmine.
Autumn Glow, orange-salmon, buff edge.
Bird of Passage, white, tipped with carmine.
Colossus, large yellow.
Carnation striped, buff, striped with crimson and lilac.
Charivari, yellow striped and blotched with carmine.
Conqueror of the whites, purest white.
Duchess of Cambridge, pink, edged with crimson.
Ebene, rosy-buff, mottled with white.
Gem, scarlet, tipped with white.
Glowing Coal, crimson-scarlet.
Hebe, white, edged with yellow, tipped with red.
Koh-i-noor, canary-yellow.
Maude, white, tipped with lilac.
Murillo, salmon, shaded lilac and carmine.
Oullet Parfait, buff, striped with scarlet.
Queen Mab, scarlet tipped with white.
Striata, lilac, striped with maroon.
Talisman, rose, striped with crimson.
Tiger, maroon-purple.
Startler, maroon, tipped with white.

Select List of Liliputian or Pompone Dahlias.

Arndt, magenta, with brown stripes and spots.
Alba Floribunda nana, pure white, very dwarf.

Black Diamond, maroon.
Guiding Star, pure white, fimbriated.
Exquisite, rich golden yellow, tipped with scarlet.
Kind and True, straw-color, tipped with purple.
Little Nymph, white, shaded with rose.
Little Kate, dark crimson.
Little Willie, richest deep pink.
Little Agnes, brightest of scarlets.
Little Dear, blush, marbled with white.
Little Herman, the finest Liliput Dahlia in cultivation; cherry-pink, tipped with white.
Otto Weilbacher, yellow, striped with scarlet.
Rachel, salmon, tipped with crimson.
Rose of Gold, finest vermillion.
Tansenblitz, deep maroon, shaded with rose.
Utz, dark maroon.

Tuberoses.

One of the most beautiful of all the summer-flowering bulbs, and unequaled in fragrance by any flower that grows. The flowers are in much request upon all festive occasions, and are also in use for funeral wreaths, crosses, etc. It is said that a million of roots are grown about the environs of New York, and they can be purchased from a single flower, with a scented leaf of geranium, to immense dishes or baskets of them, arranged with other flowers. Fifty flowers have been raised on a single stem, but from sixteen to twenty is the average number. The bulbs never bloom but once, but numerous small offsets form round the parent root, which, if kept over winter in a dry place, not less than fifty degrees in temperature, will bloom in two years. In latitudes north of New York city, the bulbs must be started early in March, to bloom before the frost touches them. There are few plants grown in the garden which give more perfect satisfaction.

The Double Tuberose is considered the most desirable flower, but the single possesses the same delicious perfume, and blooms earlier than the double. A new variety, with variegated leaves striped with light yellow, is admired for its novelty. They bloom best in a sandy soil, well enriched with concentrated manures; Guano water, prepared as before described, will hasten their flowering, and increase the number of buds.

It can be given twice a week, if the bulbs are in the open ground or in large boxes.

The Tigridia.

The Tiger-flower, or Tigridia, is a very showy Mexican bulb, growing about eighteen inches high; its flowers are four inches in diameter, and of most gorgeous coloring, and curious form. They require the same culture as the Gladiolus; will not live out of doors in cold latitudes. There are as yet but four or five varieties, which bloom from July to October.

T. pavonia, scarlet, spotted and tipped with yellow.
T. conchiflora, orange and yellow, with black spots.
T. conchiflora grandiflora, lemon-color, spotted with crimson.
T. speciosa, orange, with deep, maroon-colored spots.

Amaryllis formosissima.

The Jacobean Lily, or Amaryllis formosissima, is a dwarf-growing plant, and each bulb will usually produce two flowers of the richest crimson-violet hue, and of remarkably beautiful form; the flowers have six petals, three erect and reflexed, and three drooping, giving the flower a peculiarly graceful appearance. If planted early, in the house or hot-bed, it will bloom in June or July. The bulbs must be preserved like those of the Tigridia.

Vallota Purpurea Superba.

This plant is of the easiest culture, and no summer flowering bulb surpasses it in richness of coloring. It is a native of the Cape of Good Hope; and its leaves do not die down after the flowering season, so it cannot be packed away like other bulbs, but must be kept at rest in the earth, in a dry state. The leaves are flat and of a rich green, and spread out like a fan. The flower stalk rises about a foot in height, and bears a cluster of from six to eight scarlet, lily-shaped flowers. The bulbs are increased by numerous offsets, which will bloom in three years, at the latest. Botanists class this flower with the genus Amaryllis, and it is called in some books Amaryllis speciosa; but it is more commonly known as Valotta purpurea, though there is no shade of purple about it, for the flowers are of the brightest scarlet, with bright yellow stamens and anthers. The bulbs can be planted out in the open border, and repotted when the frost comes. It is such a showy and elegant plant, that it should be cultivated by all who delight in Flowering Bulbs.

Tritoma Uvaria Grandiflora.

This is a splendid plant, with a magnificent spike of rich orange-red flowers; from its glowing color it has been called "Red Hot Poker." It will bloom freely in any good garden soil, and is hardy in the latitude of New York city, but farther north, the roots require to be kept in sand during the winter. The flower-stem will often grow from four to five feet in height, and it produces a very fine effect. To bloom before the frost, they require to be started in March or April, and should not be planted out until there is settled warm weather.

The Summer Flowering Bulbs form a distinct class of flowers, and will, of themselves, make a gloriously gorgeous garden, requiring but little attention, as their bulbous roots do not usually demand the frequent waterings that annuals and bedding-out plants must have in this hot, dry climate. These bulbs, with the exception of the Lilies which head the chapter, must be housed in the winter, in cold climates; but our southern sisters can plant them out, and they will only ask to be removed to new quarters, as their offspring multiply and crowd them out.

The florists' catalogues offer them all at small cost, and it is impossible for those who have not feasted their eyes upon their glowing beauties, to even imagine their glories!

CHAPTER XVII.

OLD FASHIONED FLOWERS.

"O, Father, Lord !
The All-beneficent ! I bless thy name,
That thou hast mantled the green earth with flowers,
Linking our hearts to nature ! The old man's eye
Falls on the kindling blossoms, and his soul
Remembers youth and love, and hopefully
Turns unto Thee, who call'st earth's buried germs
From dust to splendor; as the mortal seed
Shall, at thy summons, from the grave spring up,
To put on glory, to be girt with power,
And fill'd with immortality."

" Common in old country gardens," is the term we often hear applied to flowers that are a little old-fashioned; yet to many hearts they are very dear. Not all the boasted glories of Verbenas, Coleus, Achyranthus, and all the newer kinds of bedding-out plants can wean us from the flowers our grandmothers loved to cherish. Their colors, markings and veinings may be far surpassed by the flowers of the present day, yet loved hands once tended them; bright eyes grew brighter at the sight of them; and they are associated with all that is holy, pure, and of good report. Who does not like to remember the days of childhood, when the gathering of old-fashioned flowers in grandmother's garden was one of the highest pleasures of life ? Cowper says, that "it is a pity that a kitten should ever become a staid, old cat," and there certainly are individuals who are tempted to wish that they had ever continued to be children. Do you remember the delicious fragrance of the white Lilac bushes that grew beside the door step, at the old farm house, and the handsful of Lilies of the Valley, that you used to gather under the old pear trees, beside the garden beds, where grew Sweet Rocket, Violets, Columbines, Spiderwort, Fleur de Luce, Daffodils, Sweet Williams, Gilliflowers, Larkspurs, Lychnis, and Nasturtiums, bright as butterflies? To be sure you do, and never will forget them while memory serves to furnish pictures for the mind's eye to view. Perhaps you gathered them to adorn a fair sister, when she gave her hand to the lover whom all considered tried and true; or, with fast dropping, blinding tears, they were plucked to wither in the chilling embrace of the reaper, Death, who had gathered the fairest flower of the hearthstone—the dearly loved baby—the youngest of the home circle! All these associations, and hundreds of others, are linked to the "old-fashioned flowers" of the past; so let us make room for them in the garden, and cherish them fondly for the sake of those who once loved them so well.

I have a great fondness for the older annuals and hardy perennials, which are now too often despised and neglected; many of them are certainly more beautiful than those which are so much praised.

A well-pruned "Snowball," in full bloom, is surely a thing of beauty! And I am certain that there are many discarded flowers which would amply repay cultivation.

The tendency of the age is to run after all that is rare and new, and to neglect that which every one possesses, forgetting the divine command to the chief of apostles, not to despise anything that God had made, nor to esteem it common. The first Dandelion possesses a great charm to me, is always gathered, and kept in water as long as a trace of its beauty remains. If it were a rare Japanese or Chinese novelty, how we should cherish it! but, no, it grows commonly by the road side, and in every pasture, so we pass it by.

There is no sweeter flower than the old, neglected Wall-flower, yet who cultivates it now? A recent writer says: "These old-fashioned flowers have a sweet fragrance which does not belong to modern favorites; and however much the last may delight us, they do not make us call to mind those delightful passages of our older poets that made our imaginations paint scenes of simple rural, floral beauty and loveliness that no artistic pencil can realize; but these 'old ladies' flowers,' or 'flowers of the poets,' often unveil to us some lovely picture or scene that long since, in our earlier readings, we had painted in the chambers of our heart, and from which memory, thus assisted, removes a pile of rubbish that had well nigh buried it in oblivion."

So we plead for the "flowers of the poets." They are all of easy cultivation, requiring little care, and blooming in endless profusion and beauty, and possessing a charm and loveliness fully equal to those which their modern sisters lay claim to.

To be sure the Tiger Lily, which was supposed to be the

"Emblem of human pride that fades away,
Of earthly joy that blooms but to decay,"

has been forced to feel the truth of the lines, and vacate its high estate for the more beauteous families imported from Japan; but the Hollyhock, of whom it was said,

"How high his haughty honor holds his head,"

has grown in elegance and gorgeousness of coloring, and has attained to the front rank among "florists' flowers." And the Aster and the Balsam have increased in beauty, and now take precedence of most other annuals; and the Gilliflower, like a real friend, attends us through all the vicissitudes and alterations of a century, even growing more beautiful. But the Marigold is almost superseded by its more brilliant sister, Tagetes signata pumila, which, in spite of its high-sounding name, is nothing but a single Marigold.

But if we read the seedsmen's catalogues attentively, we shall find the seeds of all of these "old-fashioned flowers" advertised, and can supply ourselves with a goodly show of them.

CHAPTER XVIII.

VEGETABLES—WHAT SHALL WE PLANT? HOT-BED—ITS
CULTURE, ETC.

The changes which the art of the florist has produced in double and variegated flowers, are not to be compared with the effects of cultivation on vegetables which have been for ages man's peculiar property. In their wild state, they are now scarcely recognizable.

From the Colewort, whose scanty leaves do not weigh half an ounce, come the sixty pound cabbages which are often seen in the markets. From a small, bitter root, comes the potatoes, Early Rose and Peerless, which exhibit the wondrous changes which have been wrought in them. And so on to the end of the catalogue of vegetables! What encouragement do not these facts afford to the cultivator who desires to make improvements in some classes of vegetables. If he is a benefactor to his race who can make two blades of grass grow in the place of one, surely he is one who gives to us a "Trophy" Tomato or a Brezee's "Peerless!"

Leigh Hunt, speaking of vegetables, says:—

"What a perpetual reproduction of the marvelous is carried on by nature, and how utterly ignorant we are of the causes of the least and most disesteemed of the commonest vegetables; and what a quantity of life and beauty, and mystery, and use, and enjoyment is to be found in them, composed out of all sorts of elements, and shaped as if by the hands of fairies! What workmanship, with no apparent workman! What consummate elegance, though the result is but a radish or an onion!"

The care and oversight of the vegetable as well as the flower garden, frequently devolves upon women, and as it costs no more time and labor to grow the most choice kinds, I propose to give a selection of the varieties which are the best for home culture.

The seedsmen's catalogues present us with numerous varieties, which appear quite bewildering, but I have long cared for home vegetables, and have learned what are the most desirable for my table.

In buying your seeds, do not depend upon those purchased from peddlers' carts, or from country stores; they are not so certain to be pure and fresh. Seeds from selected stocks are far superior to those gathered at hap-hazard from fields and gardens. So be sure, and provide yourself with a catalogue from a reliable source, and send thither for all you may desire.

Asparagus heads the list of early vegetables; it is almost the first green thing to show itself in the spring. Conover's Colossal is very superior to the common kinds; it will frequently send up from twenty to twenty-five stalks, as large as a man's thumb, from one plant. But it requires high culture, and much room to do this. The plants should be set three to four feet apart each way, and be thoroughly manured, and salted in November. Early in March and April, the soil should be stirred up with a three-pronged iron hand-fork. Thus treated, you can grow Asparagus as fine as any seen in Fulton market, New York.

Bush Beans.

The Newington Wonder and the Refugee have been my dependence; but last season I tried the Dwarf Wax—a waxen-yellow, stringless pod, and consider it far ahead of any other kind for table use. It makes a delicious dish—nearly equal to green peas. Among Pole Beans, the Lima is not surpassed by any other kind; but in northern New England the summers are too short to grow it in perfection, so I substitute the Dutch Case-knife, which is hardy and productive. Butter Beans are also very good, making the best succotash of any kind of Bean.

Giant Wax Beans will keep up the supply of string beans until frost comes; their waxy yellow, succulent pods, if stripped up in small bits, and boiled two hours, will provide a most excellent dish for the table, for many weeks.

Beets.

Early Flat Bassano has been the earliest variety grown; but the Dark Red Egyptian Beet has proved to be ten days earlier than any other. Its color is of the deepest red, and its flavor delicious.

The Swiss Chard, or Sea-Kale Beet, is a very desirable vegetable, as its leaves can be boiled for greens all the season. The thick, white midribs of the leaves are said to be a good substitute for Asparagus. If cut frequently, the leaves keep shooting up afresh until autumn.

Cauliflower.

The best early variety is the Early Erfurt, a compact, dwarf kind. Le Normand is of much larger growth, and later in blooming.

These vegetables should have a place in every garden, and it is vastly superior to the cabbage. Dr. Johnson, of literary fame, pronounced it the finest flower that ever bloomed.

Cabbage.

The Early Jersey Wakefield is considered the best among the early kinds, as it rarely fails to head. Early Winningstadt is the best for intermediate use; and the Premium Flat Dutch is considered unequaled for winter use. The Green Globe Savoy is the most tender, and the finest flavored, as a general rule; the larger the head of cabbage, the coarser is its flavor.

Be sure and plant some cabbages for winter salad. They are unsurpassed for this purpose, and are far more nutritious if eaten uncooked.

Cucumbers.

Early Russian Cluster is the earliest kind one can grow; but their flavor is not equal to the Early White Spine, and the pickles made from the latter, are superior. The Long Green Prickly is the firmest and best flavored; but will not be ready for the table as soon as the others.

Celery.

This vegetable demands more attention. It can be easily raised by growing in rows, and blanching in ridges, if trenching is too much trouble.

Incomparable Dwarf White is the first; of a very dwarf habit, and solid. Boston Market is very fine; White Solid is also desirable for its large size, and crisp, fine flavor.

Carrots.

One must have a bed of these for seasoning soups, and for the feathery green leaves to mingle with dishes of flowers, and vases.

Bliss' Improved Long Orange is a great improvement on the older kinds; is better flavored, and of the richest color. Large White Belgian is fine for those who like the vegetable served like squashes.

Corn.

Farmer's Club Sweet possesses a delicious flavor; very tender and sweet.

Moore's Early Concord Sweet is a new variety, obtained from crossing Crosby's Early with Burr's Improved, and is said to be unsurpassed by any other kind, either early or late. Trimble's Sugar is a very fine variety for late purposes.

Egg Plant.

Pekin New Black is a variety from China, which grows to the height of two feet, with very ornamental foliage; the fruit weighs from three to six pounds; it is very prolific, and of delicious flavor, decidedly superior to any other kind known. Seed must be sown in a hot-bed, in cold climates.

Kohl Rabi, or Turnip-rooted Cabbage.

This vegetable is a cross between a Turnip and a Cabbage in its flavor and makes a nice dish. The Early White Vienna is the best variety.

Lettuce.

The Early Curled Simpson is the best for spring use, and is largely grown in the neighborhood of New York. The Large Curled India is better for later use; it does not run to seed so quickly as other kinds, and will bear the sun better. The Green Paris Cos is the best of these varieties. Dickson's "All the Year Round" is a valuable novelty.

Melons.

Skillman's Fine Netted takes first rank; and for later use, the White Japan, Pine Apple and Green Citron are the best.

Black Spanish Water Melon is of a thin rind, and rich flavor. Mountain Sprout is a larger and later variety.

The Long Persian, imported by Bayard Taylor, is a great acquisition to the middle and southern States; is very large and of the most delicious flavor.

Joe Johnston Water Melon is also very desirable at the south; its flesh is deep red, and remarkably rich.

Okra.

The Improved Dwarf Green is better for home culture than the common variety usually grown; it is also earlier, and is equally productive. The green pods of this vegetable are used in making the famous "Gumbo" of the southern States; and are always desirable for every kind of soup.

Onions.

Yellow Danvers has long held first rank for family use; but now the seedsmen offer us rare imported varieties from Italy. Early White Naples is a distinct variety, of mild flavor; often the bulbs will weigh a pound; white skins, and very tender. New Giant Rocca, of Naples, has a brown skin, delicate flavor, and bulbs were exhibited in England which weighed three and a half pounds. Large Italian Red Tripoli, flavor mild and pleasant; bulbs have grown to weigh two and a half pounds.

Peas.

Landreth's Extra Early is said to be the earliest for garden use, and the best. Philadelphia Extra Early is also desirable; but with some seedsmen only another name for Landreth's. Little Gem is very dwarf, and of fine flavor; grows only one foot high. Hundred-fold, or Cook's Favorite, is a first-class variety; early, and very prolific. Laxton's Supreme is the earliest wrinkled pea, and has the largest pods of any kind. The Champion is a late variety, but very luxuriant, and much the best family sort raised.

Parsnips.

A new variety of these vegetables, called the Student, is much sweeter, and pleasanter in flavor, than the older kinds.

Potatoes.

Early Rose is as yet unsurpassed for table purposes, both in its early ripening, and its prolificness. Peerless is decidedly the best late potato in cultivation; grows a very large size, is of pearly whiteness, and very delicious flavor; it surely is the *ne plus ultra* of Potatoes. Jersey Peach Blows are always good, but do not yield so plentifully.

Peppers.

Sweet Mountain Peppers should be grown in every garden, to flavor the pickles. Large Bell are early and not as acrid as other kinds.

Cayenne are quite small, cone-shaped, coral-red when ripe. Good for pepper sauce.

Radishes.

Of the Early Turnip-rooted varieties, the Scarlet olive-shaped and the White Turnip-rooted are the best. The Long Scarlet Short Top, and the Long White Naples, are the most desirable of the long-rooted sorts. The Rose-colored Chinese is good for winter forcing.

Spinach.

This vegetable comes so early that every garden should have a bed of it. The Flanders is the most desirable kind, its leaves are the largest and the most succulent. The New Zealand Spinach thrives best during the heat of summer.

Sweet Potatoes.

The Nansemond has been the best kind to cultivate at the north; but the Queen of the South is now considered its superior.

Squashes.

The summer varieties are the Scolloped Bush and the Crook Neck. Of the winter, the Boston Marrow is the best early sort. Yokohama is also good; but the Hubbard excels them all, and if kept in a dry place will not decay until June.

Tomatoes.

General Grant, Charter Oak, Crimson Cluster, and the Tilden have been held in high esteem; but last year the Trophy exceeded them all, and is expected to hold the first rank. The White Apple Tomato is of very delicious flavor, and desirable to be eaten raw.

Turnips.

The Red Top Strap-leaved, and the White Strap-leaved are the best white-fleshed turnips, either for early summer or winter purposes.

Among the yellow-fleshed, Robertson's Golden Ball, and Early Yellow Finland are considered the finest grained, and the most delicate flavored.

Sweet Herbs.

A bed of Sage, Sweet Marjoram, Lavender and Caraway must not be forgotten; all of them will grow readily from seeds, if sown in beds of well-prepared garden soil. The seeds are so small, that they will not grow unless the earth is very finely pulverized.

Excepting in the middle and southern States, a hot-bed is required to start early plants, both for flower and vegetable gardens.

Boxes in the kitchen windows will do their work, but a hot-bed is by all odds the easiest method of forcing plants for early vegetables.

Directions for Making and Planting a Hot-bed.

Horse manure is the best for this purpose, because its heating properties are more intense; cow manure will do, but the growth of the plants will not be as rapid. For a week before using it, turn it over every two or three days, and if the sun is not hot enough to cause it to ferment, pour pailsful of hot water over it, the first time it is stirred up; the next time throw out all the coarsest part of the litter. When the whole heap smokes like a river on a frosty morning, it is ready for use.

Select a southeastern exposure, where the north wind will not strike upon it; a board fence at the north is a good protection. Build up the manure two or three feet in depth, and from four to six inches longer and wider than the frame. This can be made of boards fastened tightly together, and should be higher at the back than in front, so that it will present a slanting surface. Set the frame securely into the manure, leaving enough outside to bank it up well from the frost. Add four to five inches of sandy loam, thoroughly pulverized. If it can be baked in the kitchen oven, and then sifted, it will be in a perfect condition, and no weeds will grow in it. Place the sashes over it, and let it heat up for two, three or four days, according to the warmth of the sun. Put your hand in to test the soil; if it feels warm it is ready to receive the seeds. The glass is now-a-days fitted into side sashes, lapping at the edges, without transverse sash; one pane covers the other half an inch. This gives less shade upon the plants from the sashes.

Have your papers of seeds in a basket, with little sticks split at the top to hold either the printed papers or written labels; thus, when your seeds are up, you can tell an early or a late cabbage, tomato, etc. Also have a pan of common or scouring sand, well warmed in the oven. This is to scatter over the seeds, and it will make them grow more quickly than loam.

Plant your seeds in regular rows, an inch, at least, apart. Thus planted, you need not transplant all of them, some can grow in the bed all summer. Radishes should be planted three inches apart. Scatter the warm sand over the seeds, water thoroughly with a fine rose sprinkler, with warmish water; don't use cold at any time, always treat your plants to a slightly warm shower. Rain never falls chilly cold.

When thoroughly wet, spread newspapers all over them, and for two or three days sprinkle the seeds every night through the newspapers. This keeps the soil moist, and the seeds will sprout very quickly. In two days lettuce will show itself; and as soon as the tiny seedlings are up, the papers must be removed directly, else they will damp off. Planting in sods has been recommended for those vegetables which, having a top root, would not transplant readily. I have tried it with great success, with melons and cucumbers. Sods can be cut from the orchard around the apple trees, or from the road sides. Put them grass side down in the hot-bed, and plant the seeds in the soil clinging to their roots. Cover them with sand. Water and shade with papers. Squashes, Corn and Egg plants can be planted in the same way. The sods can be put into, or near a window in the barn, and the seeds will sprout soon. To transplant, the sods can be cut into pieces, and the plants in them placed in the holes prepared for them. For Melons and Cucumbers, they should be made very rich with manure; the grass will soon decay, and the vines will grow most rapidly.

Transplanting.

This should always be done after sunset. If the plants are removed at this time, they will never know that they have changed their quarters. I have transplanted tomatoes, peppers, lettuce, etc., after seven o'clock in the evening, and not a leaf has wilted the next day. Rhubarb leaves are excellent to cover young plants that are planted by daylight; they are a better protection from the sun than newspapers, as they wilt, and do not blow off.

Care of Hot-bed.

Any one can make and plant a hot-bed, but it requires more brains than a common laborer always possesses, to take care of one. One hour's neglect at noontime will scorch every tender plant; the same time, at night, may freeze it. Every morning, noon and night, it should be visited. If the night is chilly, cover it tightly with old carpets, mattings or boards; and let them remain until the sun strikes clear and warm upon the sashes. If the morning air is warm, lift the glasses a little, and by noontime admit more air. Don't keep the plants so warm that they will spindle up—nor so cool that they will chill. You must exercise your common sense, and thereby learn to keep just the right heat; a little experience will soon teach you how to manage the sashes. The weeds must not be allowed to grow, and on a sunny day when the sashes can be removed, pull them all up.

The *Gardener's Monthly* recommends the following plan for a miniature hot-bed, for raising slips in the summer time: "Get two or three boxes, eighteen inches long and ten or twelve inches wide, with a pane of glass to cover one exactly; have a hole dug deep enough, in a sunny location, to place the boxes in on a level with the ground, first taking off the bottoms of the boxes, and fitting one closely on to the other; fill up the first with fresh stable manure; in the second, place three or four inches of earth, allowing space enough between the earth and the top of the box to set in the pots and leave three or four inches of space above it; pour in a bucket of warm water, and set on the glass; let it ferment two or three days, then fill the flower pots with yellow or silver sand, and plant your cuttings; whitewash, or smear with whitening and water, the under side of the glass; set in the pots, and cover with the glass."

Of course, some of the slips will die, and they will need to be watered daily and aired. I intend to try the process this season in raising plants for window gardening.

A dry-goods box will make a good small hot-bed. Saw off the side boards and the front one, so that the sash will slide in obliquely; put cleats on all sides to support the sash; sink two feet into the ground; fill up with fermenting manure and good sandy soil, and you will find it large enough to raise tomatoes and peppers, with a large supply of flower seeds and cuttings. An old window sash can do duty for the glass. A little ingenuity will help one greatly in making hot-beds out of little material. A good kitchen garden is a capital investment for every family. It requires labor and some brains to run it — but children will often supply the former, and the housewife must not lack the latter. It should not be left entirely to the mercies of Sambo or Patrick, unless they have been well trained in its culture. As I have said before, do not expect that women can do the hard work of a garden — but they can plant the seed, and pull the weeds — if they will not let them get the start early in the season. "*One year's weeding makes seven years' seeding,*" is an old but trite proverb. Hoe up the weeds when only three or four leaves at the most are visible, and the hot sun will kill them off.

Men must take care of the paths, and prepare the soil. We, of the weaker sex, can surely do the rest—if *we please so to do*. One of the finest vegetable gardens I ever saw, was tended by a lady over sixty years of age, and so crippled, by an accident, that she could not walk without a crutch. Yet, she planted corn and cucumbers; beets and beans; potatoes and peppers; tomatoes and turnips; squashes and spinach; and her garden was always ahead of all her neighbors. She kept her beds without a weed, and her walks were as hard as if rolled — no weed dared show its tiny head long enough to mar their surface. She was a lady, delicate, refined and lovely, and her flowers and strawberries fully equaled her vegetables. Will not our fair sisters strive to imitate her example?

CHAPTER XIX.

Arrangement of Bouquets and Vases.

Flowers in Churches.

It has been said that a person must possess the "knack"— must have a taste, an eye for colors— in order to arrange flowers in bouquets, baskets, etc., artistically. And, doubtless, there is a great deal of truth in the remark. One who does possess this "knack" can walk through a garden, gathering the flowers here and there, and arranging them with a perfect blending of color, which will result in a faultless bouquet; while another, with the same flowers, fails utterly to produce a charming effect. So, one sees that the art of flower arranging is too fine and delicate to be reduced to rules. Yet, there are a few which may be of use to flower lovers who are not gifted with a truly artistic eye. All flowers will not mix readily, but are only seen in perfection when arranged by themselves. Wild flowers will not mingle tastefully with their cultivated brethren, but must be arranged by themselves. A bouquet of Laurel is very beautiful; but mingle with it the coral and topaz bells of the Columbine and you spoil its effect. And Gentians, Azaleas, May-flowers, and last, but not least, the pearly white Water Lily, are seen to the best advantage when in clusters by themselves.

Lilies of the Valley require only a background of their own green leaves, to show forth most charmingly their perfect beauty. Balsams can only be arranged in flat dishes, with a mingling of Rose Geranium leaves to add the fragrance which they lack. Sweet Peas, so soft and liquid in tint, with their exquisite rose colors, purple and browns, and pearly whites, are ruined if mingled with dazzling Geraniums or Verbenas. Put them in a tall stemmed glass, and cover them with the feathery mist of the Cliver, or Gypsophila Muralis, then they will glow like a sun-set cloud at eve.

Royal Lilies must be placed in tall vases or glasses, and Roses blend perfectly with them, while Fuchsias will droop lovingly between them.

Give Pansies and Anemones a tiny vase by themselves, and see how glorious they are. When you have a large basket of flowers to arrange, make a harmonious blending. Put the celestial blues of the Larkspurs beside the brilliant scarlets of the Verbenas and Geraniums; then add the snowy whiteness of some Phlox or Candytuft, and judge for yourself of the effectiveness of the tri-color. Yellow is very useful in the vivid arrangement of bouquets and vases. Place it beside the ruby-red Fuchsias, near to the royal purple Verbenas, and see how it enhances the brightness of their hues. Among the white Roses, mingle pink Verbenas or Geraniums; and with royal purple add cream-colored Stocks or Roses; then fill in with the neutral tints of the Mignonette, Ageratum, Heliotrope, etc., etc.,— soft and sweet — and they will heighten the contrast of the more gorgeous hues, yet do not conflict with them. A Sofrano rose bud, a sprig of Mignonette, a Tube-rose, and a bit of scarlet Verbena, mingled with Heliotrope and sweet Verbena, and some feathery green leaves, make as perfect a bouquet as one can desire to see.

If flowers could only pose themselves, it would be a great saving of trouble to many flower raisers — and doubtless the effect would be very charming.; but this pleasure is denied to them, and our ignorant fingers put them hither and thither, often in most horrid contrasts and shadings.

Remember this one rule — never put blue and purple together; never let crimson and scarlet be in juxtaposition; nor bright pink and scarlet. Arrange your flowers in shadings of the same color, or in contrasts, with a plentiful mixture of white and neutral tints. In shading flat dishes of flowers, place the darkest in the center and shade out to white.

The present fashion among florists is to arrange bouquets, baskets, etc., so as to consume as many flowers as possible; and the crowding together of such quantities produces stiffness and formality — where lightness and gracefulness should be especially sought for.

The foliage belonging to each plant is, usually, the best adapted to its peculiar beauty. The Camellia, without its leaves, is a chilly, cold flower; but combined with its rich, glossy foliage, it produces a charming effect. The contrast of their perfectly curved lines and their harmonious substance, reveal the pure beauty of the flower.

Bouquets for the hand should not be composed of solid, heavy flowers, but of those of delicate structure, and of exquisite fragrance. Such bouquets naturally undergo close inspection, and they should consist of rare ferns and bright flowers, intermingled with those that are sweet as well as lovely. Always place the most gorgeous colors in the center of bouquet, vase or basket, and shade out into perfect whiteness, relieved by green foliage.

If you desire to arrange a central piece for a dinner or supper table, at its base place the feathery leaves of ferns, lycopods, etc., and twine around the vase light, graceful vines. In the center arrange scarlet flowers, mingled with blue and white, and edge the vase with the veined leaves of the Ornamental Foliage Plants. These plants are very useful in arranging floral devices; they provide the snowy whiteness and the rich wine-red colors of flowers.

Experience is the best teacher in directing us to arrange our flowers most advantageously. And we need to heed her teachings in every department of life.

A lovely dish of flowers can be made out of soup, oyster and preserve plates. Take the largest sized deep plate your pantry will give, fill it with scouring sand, thoroughly wet; edge it with the leaves of some tricolored Geranium, or with the bright-hued Achyranthus, mingled with some white flowers—Feverfew, Candytuft, or Sweet Alyssum will do — cover the stems with another soup plate, not so large, so that the flowers and leaves will project beyond it; fill it as before directed, and edge it with some yellow flowers, Chlora, Oxura, Calceolaria—or any you can select. If the Geranium leaves were used before, mingle with these the wine-red leaves of the Variegated Plants. Proceed as before, and place on the edge of the dish bright blue Delphiniums, Blue Salvia, or the lovely Forget-Me-Not, mingled with sweet-scented Geranium leaves. In the center add a large cluster of scarlet Geraniums, Verbenas, etc., mingled with white flowers. A vase of Sweet Peas can crown the whole; and over it all, mingle the misty Cliver or Gypsophila Muralis, whose soft veil I deem indispensable. The effect is truly artistic! Purple flowers can be substituted for the blue, and you can make your own selection of colors and flowers. The fairy bells of the Fuchsias are very lovely among the silvery-edged leaves. Tropæolums mingle prettily with the darker leaves.

A dish of flowers thus arranged will be "a thing of joy" for two or three days. The sand can be wet every day with tepid water. It will make a beautiful ornament for a dinner or supper table. Flowers are always delightful when arranged in the dining room. The wise man of Queen Elizabeth's court—the immortal Bacon—never sat at his table without flowers. In his "Essays," Leigh Hunt says: "What ornament is there—what supply of light or beauty could we discover, at once so exquisite and so cheap, that should furnish our table with a grace precious in the eyes of the most intelligent?" Set flowers on your table, a whole nosegay if you can get it, or but two or three, or a single flower —a rose, a pink, even a daisy, ay, or a bunch of clover and a handful of flowering grasses, one of the most elegant as well as the cheapest of nature's productions—and you will have something on your table that will remind you of the beauties of God's creation, and give you a link with the poets and sages that have done it most honor. Put but a rose, or a lily, or a violet on your table, and you and Lord Bacon have a custom in common, for he was in the habit of having the flowers in season set upon his table, morning, noon and night. The fashions of the garments of heaven and earth endure forever, and you may adorn your table with specimens of their drapery—with flowers out of the fields and golden beams out of the blue ether.

The first new boughs in spring, plucked and put into a vase, have often an effect that may compete with flowers themselves, considering their novelty; and indeed, "leaves would be counted flowers if earth had none." Does any reader fancy that to help himself to comforts like these, would be "trifling"? Oh, let him not so condescend to the ignorance of the proud or envious. If this were trifling, then was Bacon a trifler, also the great Condé, and the old republican Ludlow, and all the great and good spirits that have loved flowers, and Milton's Adam, nay heaven itself, for heaven made these harmless elegancies, and blessed them with the universal good-will of the wise and innocent.

And surely there is nothing more interesting than the world of flowers. Earth, with seemingly careless prodigality, throws them out, masterpieces of infinite finish—all different, each perfect.

Nothing in life has afforded so much delight to so many hearts; and nothing has gladdened and brightened so many eyes!

Cutting and Preserving Flowers.

Flowers should never be cut during the intense heat of the day, but either while wet with dew in the early morn, or after sunset, when the falling dew has revived them.

Do not break them off harshly, but cut them with a knife or scissors; the former is the best, as it cuts the cleanest, and does not lacerate the minute tubes which draw up the water that nourishes the flower; if these pores or tubes are closed up the flower soon withers. I find sand far cleaner to place them in than pure water; that soon becomes disagreeable, while the sand can be thoroughly wet every morn, and keep for weeks with no unpleasant odor about it. If flowers are desired to be kept a great while, the ends of the stalks should be cut off a little every time you change the water, and a pinch of saltpetre and salt tends to prevent their decay. Soap suds, which have been widely recommended, spoil the flowers very quickly. Warm water will revive wilted flowers; put the bouquet into water warm to the hand, let it remain for an hour or more, then cut off the stalks a little and put into fresh warm water, only lukewarm, and they will brighten wonderfully.

A few drops of liquid ammonia added to the water are said to revive faded flowers, but I have never tried the remedy.

If sand cannot be obtained, put a few bits of charcoal in the water, or fill the vase with them and water, and put the stalks between them; add fresh water every day, turning out the old, and your flowers will keep a week or more. Never turn ice water into the vases, it chills the life out of the flowers—is murder in the first degree. To be sure, the ice pitcher is always at hand, but keep its contents away from your vases. Rain water is always the best for watering plants, or for keeping fresh flowers, and it should be given a little warm, even if the tea-kettle has to be resorted to to render it so.

While gathering flowers, don't pick such quantities that some will wither before they can be placed in water. If you have too many to care for directly, put them on a tray and sprinkle them with water, then they will not wither and become limp. Geranium leaves once withered never regain their fresh beauty, and Pansies once curled up will never unroll in perfect loveliness. Don't be chary of picking your flowers— the more you gather the more you will have. Give them to all your friends—a bounteous giver is always rewarded. In selecting vases, don't buy the gorgeous flowered china ware, or the brilliant Bohemian glass, but the pure, transparent glass that shows the twining stems of the flowers, and the ivory white Parian marble, around which the graceful vines will clasp so tenderly.

Silver and bronze are always beautiful, but a tasteful straw basket, holding a glass dish filled with flowers, will often produce as lovely an effect as the precious metals.

Flowers in Churches.

In adorning the Communion Table or the Font with flowers, we should select those that are bright and gorgeous, as such colors were used by the artists of the middle ages, and from time immemorial there has been a symbolism, especially in religious ceremonies and decorations. Red is the symbol of Divine love; white, of Divine wisdom; yellow is a symbol of the revelation of the love and wisdom of God; blue, of Divine eternity and of human immortality.

Our Puritan forefathers, in fleeing from the persecutions and ceremonies of an established Church, cast from them all outward adornments; we, of these later days, desire to see our churches adorned with the " Green Things of the Earth," and the practice of adorning our churches with vases and baskets of flowers is becoming quite universal. I hope it will spread, until every little village church can boast of its sweet floral adornments, from the earliest May flowers of the Spring to the crosses and crowns of " Christmas Greens."

It is but little labor for several ladies in each congregation to agree to furnish the flowers. A large marble "tazza" can be purchased either out of the church funds, or through the benevolence of the rich of the parish. To fill these every Sunday morn with all that is lovely and sweet, cannot but be a work of love.

I recall a village church which I once attended, whose pulpit was made beautiful with large vases of Roses and Spireas, mingled with the trailing vines of the Money Wort. The old deacon brought them in, with an half-concealed air of pride, and placed them on each side of the pulpit cushion, upon which lay the Bible. His daughter arranged them from the flowers that were in season every week, and he delighted to carry her floral offering to the Lord, and lay it upon His altar.

" If there is any kind of adornment which more than another seems fitted to God's house, it is that thoughtful use of the ' Green Things of the Earth.'"

Flowers are the painted sculpturings of nature—the shapes and colors of beauty, which the Creator has lavished upon the world—and surely they can never be employed for a better purpose. In the church, flowers suggest thoughts that are in unison with the occasion, and the time and care thus bestowed on the adornment of the church are not without their reward.

Pious thoughts arise while skillful fingers are busy with the work which, as it is done for the sake of God's honor, must, from its very nature, be linked with good to all concerned in it. "Whoso offereth me praise, glorifieth me."

> "Bring flowers to the shrine where we kneel in prayer,
> They are nature's offering, their place is there!
> They speak of hope, to the fainting heart,
> With a voice of comfort they come and part;
> They sleep in dust through the wintry hours,
> They break forth in glory—bring flowers, bright flowers."

CHAPTER XX.

GENERAL MANAGEMENT OF THE GARDEN.

The Soil Best Adapted to its Growth.

The most desirable soil for flowers, particularly for Annuals, Perennials, etc., is a mellow loam, that will not bake down and crack open under the influence of hard showers and hot suns. If you do not possess a good soil, why, of course, you must do the best you can, and you can improve a stiff, clayey soil by adding sand or ashes and manure.

A flower garden must have good drainage; if water settles upon its surface, and freezes and thaws during the winter, you may be sure that your plants will not survive. There is no use in trying to grow flowers in poor soil; but every one can make a small compost heap, in an out-of-the-way corner, and give it all the soap suds on washing days that are not needed on the borders. When the leaves fall, secure all you can; hire a small boy to gather them for you, and put them on the pile; they are said to be the very poetry of manure—certainly, they contain the best elements of flower food. Add to this heap the weeds that are collected, but don't have any seed-pods among them; throw upon it all the slops from the house, and, by the next year, you will have good plant food. It must be turned over several times so as to expose it to the action of the air. A load of grass sods from the meadow is the best foundation for such a "bank." To use this season, procure a large barrel, and fill it up with as good soil as your garden can boast, then turn into it, every morning, the slops from the chambers. No disagreeable odor will arise from it, but a rich soil will be made. Use it carefully, putting a few tablespoonsful about the roots of the plants, and digging them in, so as not to touch the stems. Dig this about the roots of your Geraniums, Roses, Verbenas, Pansies, etc., not letting it come in direct contact with the tender roots, and you need not complain of the poverty of the soil; while the rich blooms of your flowers will fully repay the extra labor. The barrel can be hid away under vines; and, as the earth is used up, add more to it. The Japanese and Chinese gardeners can teach us a lesson in these matters. Nothing is wasted in their country and their flower gardens are wonderfully beautiful and gorgeous.

"Eternal vigilance," Gen. Jackson's pet phrase, applies particularly to gardening. One cannot grow fine flowers without some labor; and you will soon learn that constant efforts are needed to make the flowers grow into fine-shaped plants, filled with blossoms. You cannot garden one week, and let it alone the next; but you must watch it, and water it, and weed it, daily, if you would be successful. It requires as much care to cultivate a handsome garden, as to grow cabbages, melons and tomatoes, and no more.

An open exposure is desirable, where the sun will have free access to the plants; there are some flowers like Fuchsias, Primroses, Daisies Pansies, etc., which bloom far better in beds that are sheltered from the noonday sun; and their tastes should be gratified. Yet nearly all plants love the sun, and grow better, if directly under its influence.

Selection and Sowing of Seeds.

This is a matter of importance to amateur gardeners, who usually desire the handsomest kinds that can be grown. It takes no more time and care to grow a small, poor, single flower than a rich, double variety; and the cost is but little more. Always purchase your seeds of reliable, well-known seedsmen, and do not content yourself with those offered by small traders.

Seed raisers who make it a business, raise only the finest kinds; the poorer sorts do not pay. Hundreds of dollars worth of good seeds are annually wasted because the growers do not know how to plant them. They require a very finely pulverized soil; and, if the coarser particles are sifted out, the seeds will germinate more surely. In the Chapter on ANNUALS, minute directions are given for sowing seeds. Since writing it, I have sowed sixty, or more, different varieties, and hardly one has failed to germinate. Every seed of some varieties has come "up." There is no difficulty in their culture, if you will only take a little pains in planting them, and shield them from the sun, with newspapers, for two or three days.

Weeding.

This is usually considered a terror; but if you will use a small rake and hoe, as heretofore advised, *every morning*, for a few minutes, you will keep the upperhand of them. The first leaves of weeds or plants are their sole nourishment; cut them off and the young weeds must die, however tenacious of life they may be.

Watering.

Leaves absorb and give out moisture, and inhale and exhale air; they are the lungs of every plant, and if they are destroyed the whole plant suffers. The pores in the leaves of all plants, by which they transmit air and moisture, are exceedingly small, and liable to be filled up if exposed to smoke and dust; therefore, if there are not plentiful showers, you must water them freely every evening. It is of but little use to give water after the sun has risen. In this hot, dry climate the watering pot is a necessity, and tubs of water should be drawn from hydrant or pump every morning, and allowed to set in the sun, to take off the chill; then, after seven o'clock P. M., apply it.

Planting Out, Pruning, etc.

The branches and leaves of plants rarely touch one another while growing, and you should learn from them not to crowd your plants in bed or border; for air and light are quite as needful as water and good soil.

When shrubs produce an abundance of foliage and no flowers, either remove them to a purer soil, or cut through some of the principal roots. Root-shortening is often resorted to, by florists, to force plants to bloom.

By checking the growth of plants, you throw strength into the flowers. All shrubs produce their flowers on the terminal points of the branches; after the bloom is past, if these are pinched off, you will have two or three branches for one in the succeeding year.

All plants are in their most vigorous growth while in flower, and should never be transplanted at that time, for it will check their growth, if it does not kill them. This is the time for taking cuttings, as they are then most ready to send forth roots. The throwing off of its leaves by a newly planted cutting, is a sign that it has begun to grow, while if the leaves wither on the stem, it shows that the cutting had not strength enough to send forth shoots.

You can train a plant into any shape you please, by pinching off the shoots, for the plant will avenge itself by sending forth two or three more, in lieu of the one you pinched in. A plant pinched in June will flower in July; if pinched in July, it will flower in August. All buds proceed from the tips, and by pinching in Carnations, Bouvardias, Fuchsias, etc., their flowers will be put back and they need not be allowed to bloom until autumn. This method of training will produce thick, bushy plants, filled with many small shoots, which, when left unmolested, will produce hundreds of buds and flowers.

To procure a succession of Roses, prune down to three eyes on all the branches of some bushes, as soon as the buds begin to expand; defer the same operation with others, until the leaves are expanding; on the former bushes the three buds will bear early flowers; in the latter, they will not begin to expand until the others are in full foliage, and will bloom later in the season.

Dry, east winds are very injurious to plant life, by absorbing the moisture from the leaves of the plants more quickly than they are able to give it out; they will often wither the plants as badly as a frost, and should be guarded against in the same way. Cover all your plants with papers, boxes, etc., if they are so unfortunate as to be exposed to it. I have seen an east wind nearly ruin a flourishing bed of Verbenas and Heliotropes in the month of May. If your grass-plat becomes overrun with moss, manure the surface, and the grass will soon catch in and expel the intruder.

Plants, when in bloom, have all their juices in the most perfect state; therefore cut all aromatic and medicinal herbs just as they begin to send up flowering stalks.

Profuse flowering exhausts the strength of plants; therefore remove all seed pods that are not especially desired for seed. Do this to all perennials, and you will have much finer blossoms the ensuing season.

Saving of Seeds.

Though the gathering of seeds reminds us that the beauty of the flower is gone, it is a pleasing occupation, because it promises us pleasure for another year. As an usual thing it is better to depend upon the seedsmen for your supply, but if you have very fine flowers, choose two or three plants and pick off all the side buds, sending the whole strength of the plant into two or three blossoms at the most; frequently one is quite enough. Tie up the plants with colored yarn, so that no one will pick them; pull up all the single flowers that might mix with them, and you may be quite sure of saving good seed. Gather them on a dry day, when the seeds are thoroughly dry. Seeds preserved in the seed vessel are more clumsy to pack away than those which are cleaned, but they are said to keep fresher. When ready to sow them, clean them by passing them through sieves, having holes large enough to let the dust escape and retain the seeds. Small sieves can be made of a thin bit of pasteboard cut in a circular form, and the edges turned up, then pierce the bottom of it with holes made with a pin or a darning needle. Make several different sized sieves, and rub the seeds through the different ones·

A lady can make a small cabinet of pasteboard, with as many drawers in it as there are letters of the alphabet, and as she ties up the packets, each can be put into its corresponding drawer; or a paper bag with each letter of the alphabet marked upon it, can hold the seeds until desired for planting.

Preparing Pots.

If new pots are used for any kind of seeds or plants, they should be soaked in water for a few hours, as they will otherwise suck away the moisture from the earth, and nothing is worse than to water seeds too often, or let them become dried up. All empty pots should be washed and cleaned before using again.

Taking up and Preserving Flowers in Winter.

One is often in a great quandary to know what to do with large bushes of Geraniums, Roses, Feverfews, Heliotropes, etc., that have grown so finely all summer, and now the frost threatens to lay them low forever·

All the plants that have a woody nature, can be preserved in a dry, cool, perfectly dark cellar. Last autumn, I had a splendid bed of Zonale Geraniums—every color and hue, and some fifteen plants. What should I do with them? I could not bear to lose them forever! So I took a large box, and filled it with a light soil, and planted the roots in it, first cutting off all the tender branches, and leaving none over twelve or fifteen inches long; on these the leaves were left, but every blossom was cut away. The box was placed in a cold, damp, perfectly dark cellar, where potatoes never freeze; no water was given it the whole winter, and the first of May it was brought up with every root alive. The leaves had all fallen, and the stems were dead down three or more inches. I cut them back six inches, and bright leaves are now starting from every branch.

I live in the coldest climate in New England, where one has to fight for flowers or fruits. "Nine months of winter, and three months of spring," describes the rigorous climate, and all Roses excepting the tender *Teas*, will live under sods. They are cut from the meadows or road sides early in November; then the bushes are carefully laid down; and the sods are placed over them grass side up. Last winter there was but little snow, but my roses kept finely. A large shovelful of manure was thrown around the roots before the branches were laid down, As the sods were being placed over the Roses, I laid a small piece over two Feverfews that grew near, and they are both alive. They will live out in milder climates, but are rarely known to do so in this frigid zone, under Mt. Washington's shadow. Fuchsias and Heliotropes can be kept in boxes in the same manner. Also Oleanders, Sweet Verbenas, and nearly all flowers but Verbenas; they require light, heat and moisture to live.

Zonale Geraniums can be wintered in most cellars, if the earth is shaken from the roots, and they are tied up by them to the beams of the cellar. All blossoms should be cut off, or the sap that is in the branches will cause them to bloom, and thus rob the roots of the strength they need to live on through the winter. A damp cellar will cause them to decay. Scarlet Salvias can be kept in the same way.

Roses and Geraniums, etc., can be buried in trenches. Dig it two and a-half feet in depth, and where the water will not settle; lay in the plants, first throwing in a few shovelsful of dried leaves, or boards can be laid over the plants; fill in with sandy loam, and finish off with a ridge that will carry off the water. If the trench is lined with straw before the plants are laid in, they are less liable to decay. It is no use trying to make "window gardens" out of plants that have flowered all summer. They must have a season of rest, and they are only desirable for another summer after they have slept away the winter in the cool, dark cellar.

Sleep of Flowers.

It is said that nearly all flowers sleep at night. The Marigold goes to sleep with the sun, and awakes at its bidding. The Dandelion shuts tightly its bright blossoms before nine in the evening, and does not fully open them until at six in the morning. The Daisy closes its flowers in the evening, and opens its "day's eye" to meet the earliest beams of the rising sun. The Goat's Beard wakes at three in the morning, and goes to sleep by five or six in the afternoon. The Crocus, Tulip and many others sleep peacefully at night. The Ivy-leaved Lettuce awakes at eight in the morn, and closes forever by four in the afternoon. The Night Blooming Cereus turns night into day; it expands its magnificent fragrant chalices in the twilight, is fully blown at midnight, and sleeps never to awake again at the dawn of the morning. In a Clover field, not a leaf opens until touched by the sun's rays. An English florist has closely watched the habits of the flowers, and thus reports concerning them.

Insects.

Insects abound in every month of the year, but they are especially annoying in Summer time. With the first warm days they appear in numbers, and cover the Roses, etc. Rain causes them to disappear, but a dry, east wind increases them. A small painter's brush, dipped in quassia or aloes water, will brush them off and destroy them.

The caterpillars of many moths and butterflies are destructive in the garden, and one death in the Spring will save much warfare; so if you see one resting on a stem or leaf, with folded wings, it is probably a female and should be killed directly. If one is found dead on a plant, she has doubtless laid her eggs, and you must search for them underneath the leaves and burn them. A garden syringe or engine is the best weapon with which to wage warfare against both aphides and caterpillars. You must hold the pipe close to the plant, and pump hard, so as to bring a considerable stream upon it, and it will soon be free from them. Every time you use it, you should rake the earth away from under the plants, and trample upon the insects you have washed off.

Earwigs are very destructive insects. Their favorite food is the petals of roses, pinks, fuchsias, dahlias, etc. They eat at night, and in the daytime hide away in the dark vegetation. They can be caught by driving stakes into the ground and inverting a flower-pot directly over them, leaving just room for them to crawl under, and then look for and destroy them every morning.

Grubs on orchard trees and small fruits, will sometimes spoil the whole harvest; but if a bonfire is made with dry sticks and weeds on the windward side of the orchard, the smoke will blow among the trees and destroy hundreds, while the flames will attract many moths. Make the fire after nightfall.

Wasps destroy a quantity of fruit, and all that you can kill in the spring will save a swarm in the autumn. But be careful about letting them sting you, for the smart is severe. If stung, get out the blue-bag from the laundry, and rub it well into the sting, or cover the spot with soft soap, or liquid ammonia, to neutralize the acid of the poison. Saleratus wet and rubbed on the wound will also mitigate the pain.

Cherish the little black and red lady-bug, for it will destroy many green lice, or aphides. They are often to be found on the currant bushes, and I always catch them and give them a home among my roses and geraniums.

Toads are among the best friends that we can cultivate, so be sure to treat them with kindness. They may eat a few strawberrries, but let them have that privilege in return for the immense quantities of insects they will also eat. If you can have none in your garden, it is well to seek for them in your walks, and bring them home, handling them carefully, for though they have no power to injure you, being perfectly harmless, you can easily kill them. I have a portly couple of them who live under my front door-step, and nightly come forth to feed upon my enemies—the noxious insects—eating bugs, grubs, moths, millipedes, and caterpillars.

Bees, of various kinds, are useful in spreading the pollen, so be sure to bid them welcome to all the hidden sweets your flowers contain.

Cultivate the Beautiful.

"Flowers seem intended for the solace of ordinary humanity. Children love them; quiet, tender, contented, ordinary people love them as they grow; luxurious and disorderly people rejoice in them gathered. They are the cottager's treasure, and, in the crowded town, mark, as with a little broken fragment of rainbow, the windows of the workers, in whose hearts rests the covenant of peace. To the child and the girl, to the peasant and manufacturing operative, to the grisette and the nun, the lover and the monk, they are precious always." Thus writes Ruskin, the prose poet of the century.

The cultivation of "The Beautiful" should be the desire of every woman's heart. Gœthe's sentiment, "We should do our utmost to encourage the Beautiful, for the useful encourages itself," should be our watchword. There are few women who do not take delight in flowers, and the object of this little book is to encourage them to cultivate them around and about their own homes, where their fragrance will delight every one that passes by them.

They speak to us of love and joy; of hope and peace; of humility and confidence; and also of bitter sorrow and grief — for they are associated with those who have passed away, and whose loss has darkened the horizon of our lives. They also teach us of the resurrection of the dead, and the life immortal that fadeth not away. They adorn the soldier's grave; they circle the brow of loveliness; they crown the festive hall; they are everywhere, and are closely mingled with both joy and sorrow.

They are not a necessity to many of us; but they teach us to live nearer to God. Truly Mrs. Howitt writes of them:

"Our outward life requires them not,
Then wherefore have they birth?
To minister delight to man,
To beautify the earth!
To comfort man—to whisper hope,
Where'er his faith is dim,
For whoso careth for the flowers,
Will much more care for Him!"

I truly pity those who cannot turn from the hurry of business with all its corroding cares, from the pomp of wealth, and the gay devices of fashion, and feast their senses and their souls upon the sight and perfume of a flower!

Far better to teach our daughters to cultivate roses on the cheeks, and in their gardens, to ornament their rooms with the fragrance and beauty of roses and lilies, and all the gorgeous sisterhood of flowers, than to make ruffles, and puffs, and plaits and endless puckers wherewith to adorn themselves. Children can easily be taught to love flowers, and the taste can never be used to deteriorate the character.

Linnæus, the renowned Swedish botanist, was the son of a poor country clergyman, who had a small flower-garden, in which he cultivated all the flowers which he could procure, and his means would permit.

From the earliest childhood he taught his son to love them, cultivat[e] them, and rejoice with intense delight in their rich and varied colo[r]ings. In this way he created in him the tastes and desires which mad[e] him the first botanist and naturalist of his age.

FINIS.

www.ingramcontent.com/pod-product-compliance
Lightning Source LLC
Chambersburg PA
CBHW022126160426
43197CB00009B/1170